THOSE WHO SHOW UP

It is not the critic who counts; not the person who points out how the strong man stumbles, or where the doer of deeds could have done them better. The credit belongs to the person who is actually in the arena, whose face is marred by dust and sweat and blood; who strives valiantly; who errs, who comes short again and again, because there is no effort without error and shortcoming; but who does actually strive to do the deeds; who knows great enthusiasms, the great devotions; who spends themselves in a worthy cause; who at the best knows in the end the triumph of high achievement, and who at the worst, if they fail, at least fail while daring greatly, so that their place shall never be with those cold and timid souls who neither know victory nor defeat.

From a speech given by the former President of the United States, Theodore Roosevelt at the Sorbonne in Paris, France, on 23 April 1910

THOSE WHO SHOW UP

Andy Flannagan

Muddy
Pearl

First published in 2015 by
Muddy Pearl, Edinburgh, Scotland
www.muddypearl.com
books@muddypearl.com

British Library Cataloguing in Publication Data
A catalogue record for this book is available from the British Library.

ISBN   978 1 910012 19 2

Typeset in Minion by Waverley Typesetters, Warham, Norfolk
Printed by Nørhaven, Denmark

To Jen and Jesse
I am so very glad that you showed up.

ACKNOWLEDGEMENTS

This book is written by me, but large chunks of it could not have been written without these wonderful fellow-travellers: David Landrum, Colin Bloom, Claire Mathys, Maeve Sherlock, Zoe Dixon, Elizabeth Berridge, Justin Brierley, Kieran Turner, David Barclay, Martyn Casserly and Jack Palmer.

Thanks also to my ever-supportive executive and the wonderful Rob Carr. Thanks to Mark Scott for logistical support. Thanks to Andy Reed for being a hugely important part of my journey.

Thanks to Stephanie Heald for the provocation to get on and write this book. But also thanks for putting your money where your mouth is and editing it. I cannot understand your patience and thoroughness, but I am so very thankful for them!

CONTENTS

FOREWORD

The Archbishop of Canterbury, Justin Welby

Upon entering politics, Charles de Gaulle is reported to have remarked: 'I have come to the conclusion that politics are too serious a matter to be left to the politicians.' This is the sentiment that can be found in this book. It is a robust call for us – all of us – to re-engage, or in some cases participate for the first time, in the political world. This is not a book about supporting any one party, but about encouraging people to engage with politics deeply and critically, as a means of shaping our life together.

There are many reasons why people, particularly amongst the younger generations, choose not to engage with politics. Disaffection with those who have been elected to represent us, pessimism about the prospects of anything changing, the complexities of life simply taking priority over getting to the ballot box or the local council meeting. These are all valid reasons for scepticism, but not for apathy.

Andy Flannagan's call to action, in tandem with the important work of Christians in Politics and the 'Show Up' campaign in the run up to the General Election, is challenging and encouraging in equal measure. It is built on a deeply Biblical understanding of what it means to be a follower of Christ – the tour through what the Bible has to say about engaging in what we today call politics is impressive. Andy is reaching out, inspiring and equipping us to become engaged with a system that affects us deeply, and through which we in turn can effect radical and transformational change across our society.

This is not to say that we will all agree with everything Andy writes in *Those Who Show Up*. Politics would be extremely dull if we all agreed on everything. There is joy in diversity, and we should not be afraid to disagree with one another, but in a way that models the reconciling love of Jesus. Good disagreement is a gift that the church can offer the world around it – and our political system could certainly do with a healthy dose of it.

The stories that Andy tells in *Those Who Show Up* are testament to his experience of political activism, particularly the work done in partnership with his co-Directors at Christians in Politics, who between them represent the Christian groups affiliated to the Conservative, Labour and Liberal Democrat parties.

The growth of this organisation is good news – not least because it is drawing people in from across the political and theological spectrum. The 'kingdom first' approach that is front and centre of the organisation's approach to politics, and which Andy articulates most persuasively in this book, is where political engagement should start – casting our ballot in an election or standing for election only make sense in a context of thoughtful reflection.

There are many aspects of modern life that seem to pull us away from a concern for each other's well-being. Christians must be actively concerned with the pursuit of the common good and the flourishing of all in our society – be it local, national or global. The most practical way of doing this is through the political process in its broadest sense. Church people are better placed to do this than they often realise. We are usually very involved in the community, have good relationships with a wide range of people and institutions and can mobilise people on important issues. We have what they call in the business, leverage.

We must go into the political arena with our eyes open, because it can be a difficult place to live within. Andy fully recognises the traps and pitfalls that we may encounter, but also offers encouragement and support for how we can live authentic and politically-engaged lives.

I do hope that you will *show up*.

Justin Welby, London, 2015.

INTRODUCTION

In the second series of the animated TV show *The Simpsons* there is a fascinating episode called 'Lisa's Substitute'. It includes an amusing subplot set in her brother Bart's classroom in which he and his classmates must elect a class president. Their teacher, Mrs. Krabappel, nominates the outstanding pupil Martin Prince, while Sherri and Terri nominate the less-than-outstanding Bart. During a 'presidential debate' Bart tells a series of infantile jokes which win the support of his classmates, much to the disgust of Martin who wants to focus on 'the issues'. Bart is buoyed by the frenzied adulation like a teenage pop sensation. The groundswell is so overwhelming that Bart is obviously going to win by a landslide. He is, in fact, so confident of his victory that he does not even bother to vote. However his huge confidence has spread to his wide-eyed followers, who similarly do not feel the need to turn up at the ballot box. In fact the only kids who do vote are Martin (who votes for himself) and Wendell Borton (who also votes for Martin). Nobody had predicted that the kid famed for his nerdiness and nausea would be the kingmaker!

The point here is not whether Bart should have been elected class president. This is not Florida and the year is not 2000. The point is also not whether Bart would have made a better class president than Martin (I think we all know the answer to that one). The point is that the firmly held opinions of Bart's classmates counted for nothing because they did not show up.

There is a difference between holding an opinion and actually expressing it. Then there is a further difference between just expressing that opinion out into the ether, and formally standing by it in something like an election. You can wish me 'Happy Birthday' on Facebook all you like, but it will mean an awful lot more to me if you actually show up at my party in person. One action takes three tenths of a second and the other takes considerably longer. Much of our modern-day campaigning is effectively cost free. We click and share a good cause and that's that. This book is about the intriguing discipleship and adventure that happens when what we believe starts to cost us something in terms of time, effort or reputation. Sorry – I hope you weren't expecting a slick sales pitch.

'Hang on, is this another book telling me how important it is to vote?' I can already hear you saying, 'But there isn't anyone I want to vote for – I am not impressed by any of the parties'.

Tell me about it. No, this isn't another book trying to convince you to do that. It isn't trying to get you to vote. It's going to suggest that you could be voted for. It's going to suggest that it could be your name on the ballot paper. Or that you could be helping someone whose name is. It's going to suggest that, in one small way, Martin Prince could be your role model for life.

People are hugely unimpressed with politics and politicians. This book will delve into some of the reasons for this, but will also point in the direction of some remedies. The passion expressed in the Scottish referendum campaign in 2014 showed that people do care about how their countries and communities are run. The question is, will we allow those thoughts to recline as mere opinions, or will we let them take a stand? All of us know the frustration of harbouring an opinion while feeling unable to express it meaningfully. In home or work contexts it usually leads to a lot of bitterness and resentment. As a nation, and especially as the church, we are in danger of sliding in that direction, unless we break out of the mindset that we will always be commentators, and never participants.

Don't just send. Be sent

A few years ago we developed a campaign based around a postcard. Written boldly at the top were the words 'Do not send this postcard'. It was aimed at a generation of Christians who had spent the last decade sending postcards. Many postcards. I was one of them. Those postcards were about all manner of important issues – like third world debt, trade rules, abortion, trafficking and climate change. They were sent to those in positions of power who we hoped would note the strength of opinion of a large number of people on the given subject. But our new postcard had no address and no space for a stamp. It simply said 'Have you ever sent a campaigning postcard? Did you hope that the person who read it had the passion to make change happen? We think YOU could be that person. Don't just send. Be sent.'

This call to apostleship was an attempt to flip our assumptions as Christians. We can be led by church culture to believe that any leadership gifting we may have is primarily designated for leading within the four walls of the church, rather than in society at large. We may pay lip service to the idea of Christians leading 'out there', but our church culture often screams the opposite. I grew up wanting to be a worship leader partly because I saw lots of worship leaders heralded. I also grew up wanting to work for Christian organisations because it was their leaders and work that were held up to me as examples. I wasn't exposed to too many Christian businessmen or journalists.

You don't need me to remind you that the church hasn't always been successful in influencing society with its firmly held beliefs in recent years. One reason is this lack of showing up in public leadership. We declare our opinions loudly to our own kind or on the internet, but fight shy of working with or building relationships with those who may not agree with us. Perhaps we also just don't want the responsibility of public office.

So showing up is not just about voting. Although that is obviously a good start. It's not just about making a mark on a ballot paper, but leaving your mark on society. This is about representing yourself and potentially many others. I am suggesting that your vote could just be the start of you making significant decisions, rather than the end. Will we just follow, or, in the pattern of Jesus, might we serve and lead?

Those who show up

So to the title. No one seems to be certain who first coined the famous phrase, 'Decisions are made by those who show up'. Its potential authors include a range of people from former US Presidents to movie-maker Woody Allen, and it had something of a renaissance when it was used in the American TV show *The West Wing*.

But whoever first uttered the phrase, it is hard to argue with. History is made by those who show up. It always has been. (It is also written by those who win the wars, but that's the subject for another book entirely.) Decisions are made by those who *show up*. Not necessarily the smartest, not necessarily the most qualified, not necessarily those of the best character, not necessarily those who may have gleaned some divine wisdom, but by those who, like Wendell Borton, simply show up. It is sobering, but perhaps also empowering. You don't need outrageous gifting to show up. You just need a body.

The same is true throughout the stories of Scripture. Yes, at times God moves in miraculous ways without human agency, but much more frequently he moves through one or more of his unremarkable people who seem to be in the right ordinary place at the right time. The CVs of Gideon, Moses or Rahab were not exactly screaming out for their respective jobs. They just showed up in obedience.

'Where do people show up?' I hear you cry. They show up in a variety of places which may not always be obvious. They show up at local residents' meetings. They show up at parents' associations. They show up at safer neighbourhood groups. They show up at town council meetings. They show up at political party branch meetings. You may well be one of them.

At our local Tenants' and Residents' Association, when we come to vote on, say, where to develop a new garden project, it might seem obvious that it would be best to place it in front of Tricia's flat, because there are lots of passionate gardeners nearby. But if Tricia and her friends don't turn up to the meeting, their votes cannot be counted. They can complain all they want afterwards, but the bottom line is that they weren't there. Gardens – and history – are made by those who show up.

You see, the places that these people show up are not the fun places. These places generally involve chairpersons, secretaries, treasurers and minutes. These places are generally dusty old halls. These places don't have welcome teams with Fairtrade coffee, doughnuts and biscuits, and if they do manage a biccie, it'll probably just be a Rich Tea.

But these people run the world, in the macro and the micro. There are some seriously hard yards to do. There is a lot of tiresome, repetitive work that is non-negotiable. And to get to elevated positions these people have been showing up at some pretty dull meetings for a long time. But we rarely think about that because we usually only hear about them once they've got to the top.

When we reflect on history we do try to remember those who showed up, but our focus tends to be on the endpoints rather than the starting points. We forget that in between someone forming an opinion, and the transformation of society occurring, a lot of hard work happened. The activists in the Civil Rights Movement didn't just believe racism was wrong. They showed up. The Suffragettes didn't just believe women should have the right to vote. They showed up. And it cost them. We don't often read about all the meetings that paved the way for those mass movements. And there were many of them. But they don't make great movies.

To give you an example, here is a summary of the minutes of the very first meeting of a campaign group. (Even the word 'minutes' has you dropping off, doesn't it?)

- They decided that the current law was bad and that the committee's main aim was to persuade other people of that fact, mostly by producing publications.

- They decided who could be on the committee and that the quorum would be three members – i.e. the minimum number who had to be present for a meeting to count.

- They chose one of the group to be Treasurer but then said he couldn't spend any money unless the whole committee said he could.

- They agreed to announce what they had decided, then ask other people to join and send money.

Then they adjourned and went for a drink. In fact I could still take you to that very pub. It didn't exactly feel like a dramatic start. But these were the minutes of the first meeting on 22nd May 1787 of what would become the London Abolition Committee whose aim was to make the slave trade illegal. You can sit in the British Library holding those minutes, reading the original record book. There is no getting away from the fact that the meetings sounded quite dull. But, year by year, through the leadership of folks like William Wilberforce, Olaudah Equiano, Elizabeth Heyrick and Thomas Clarkson, the campaign gathered steam, until eventually on 1st May 1807 the Bill outlawing the slave trade took effect. I think we can agree that even though it took twenty years, it was worth showing up at that first meeting.

My hope and prayer is that this book will encourage you to show up, as they did.

1

SHOWING UP: LUTON

I am proud to say that I lived, for seven-and-a-half years, in Luton. It doesn't have the best reputation in the world. A quick drop into Luton airport before heading on to London or somewhere more exotic is the extent of most folks' interaction with the place. This inevitably reinforces its image. Think quite a lot of concrete, a town centre built around a 1960s shopping precinct, and Lorraine Chase's accent, and you are getting the picture. Not exactly the Cotswolds. But I loved the place and its people.

Among the folks I knew best in Luton were some incredible youth workers. These guys had a huge heart for the town and especially its young people. Week by week I would hear about, and at times experience up close, story after story of the very beautiful but very broken young people of Luton. The level of investment my friends made into these young lives was inspiring. Like Charlie's investment into a kid called Matt. So many nights in casualty, so many false starts as the drug habit kicked in again, so much pain as he stole from the homes who took him in.

Many of these kids had what I could only describe as a reverse head start. They had been left with huge psychological scars caused by acts of omission or commission. By abusive or alcoholic parents, or by parents simply not being around. You could see all too plainly the difference this made to their interaction with others and their reactions to stressful circumstances. In their actions they called loudly for attention, having been given little in their own families. Lies planted deep in their souls about rejection or ugliness needed rewriting. These young people were impressive in their desire to persevere in the midst of these challenges, and it was a privilege to watch some beautiful transformations happen. On recognising that they were unconditionally loved, and on finding an accepting community, beautiful green shoots grew up through the concrete.

During this time I met a young guy called Gavin Shuker. Gavin was born and bred in Luton. He attended his local comprehensive school and sixth form college, and then won a scholarship to Cambridge University. There he joined a vibrant student-focused church, but felt a strong call to return home to Luton to plant a new church. He convinced a group of fellow Cambridge graduates to follow him to Luton – not the most traditional next step after Cambridge! They started a church and began to serve their community in Luton, slowly growing as a body of believers and seeking to bring the kingdom in every sphere of local life.

They got alongside homeless people, students, and those involved in the sex trade. However, before long, some of them began to realise that the individuals they were helping were in many cases the victims of dysfunctional systems and structures. Their problems were not only personal. The abuse they suffered was allowed – enabled even – because of loopholes in regulations, or lack of focus and resources in applying them. Things like regulations forcing trafficked workers into self-employment, so that they had no legal recourse to an employer. The church were waking up to the web of factors that affect a life, and they were not content to just be the ones applying the sticking plaster. Many of the decisions that were needed were made at council or national level and were therefore political decisions, so it made perfect sense for the church members to get involved politically.

As part of this, some of them joined the local Labour party. Their youthful enthusiasm and proficiency was noticed quickly, and before long Gavin was organising the website and database of the local party. Gavin was then also given a part-time job working with the sitting MP for Luton South. His leadership and communication skills were being noticed, but he had no ambitions beyond leading the church and being present in the midst of the local political world.

Then, out of nowhere, the expenses scandal of 2009 struck Westminster. One of those who had to resign was the MP for Luton South, and, after some prayer and discussion, Gavin surprised many by deciding to stand for selection to replace her. There was no dramatic call. Having been content to serve as a normal member, an opportunity had presented itself and he calculated he was in as good a position as anyone to serve his town. So he put his name forward. He was prepared to show up. There were a large number of contenders for the position and everyone was sick of the endless fliers. But no one in Luton had ever received a DVD through their door encouraging them to vote. And he was a dynamic young candidate. After an extraordinarily tight, and at times difficult battle, Gavin was selected to be Luton South's Labour parliamentary candidate.

However, that was just the start of the hard work. The antics of the departing MP had left local people angry at the Labour party, and nationally people were migrating away from Labour in sizeable numbers. But Gavin's fresh passion began to attract many folks who had previously not been involved in politics. Diehard local Labour party members were enthused by a movement of people campaigning for Gavin, some of whom weren't even party members.

To cut a long story short, the end result was that in May 2010, a 28-year-old church leader became the Member of Parliament for Luton South. Stop for a moment and take that in. The obstacles that we imagine lie in wait for us because we are Christians often just aren't there. There is no glass ceiling. The key to Gavin's success was not simply his winsome engagement, but the fact that this was an adventure that a community of people went on together. As I spent time with them during the campaign, I was continually amazed by how others joined in the adventure, and these folks were drawn from all manner of backgrounds. They were drawn to something of the kingdom. Relationships between Christians, Muslims, political, and non-political folks were forged in a way that simply would not have been possible otherwise.

But the truth is that what we are celebrating here goes much wider than just Gavin. He is what you might call the firstfruits of a generation passionate about justice – those who cried 'Jubilee!' for cancelling global debt, who marched to make poverty history, and raged against people trafficking. Now that generation are realising the importance of not just shouting from the sidelines, but getting on the pitch. The influx of passionate young people into Luton's local party changed the face of their campaign with their energy, optimism and faith.

The impact of Gavin's election has continued to cause ripples. A number of those young people who helped Gavin to get elected were inspired by his example. They could see the positive influence of his role in the town and began to realise the importance of political engagement. They have since stepped forward and been elected. People like Fiona Green (a church leader) and Andrew Malcolm (a teacher and church musician) are now also local councillors serving the town they love.

I can't say this strongly enough. They are normal church people just like you and me. There was no dramatic call to politics. There was no special preparation. They just showed up. And it has not always been easy for them, as youthful enthusiasm, creativity and energy inevitably collide with 'the way things have always been done around here'. Long established traditions – principalities and powers even – are being engaged.

I was back in Luton meeting some friends recently and it was wonderful to learn something unexpected. I chatted to some young people who talked with real pride about Gavin being their MP. For a young person to be positive about or even discuss politics is worthy of a newspaper article in itself, but this went deeper. They described how important it was that they had someone to look up to who was one of them. A youth worker explained to me that these people, who had little expectation, who were depressed about the future, now had hope. It was as if heads that had been drooping, permanently tilted downwards, were gradually being lifted up. Obviously it's not all down to one man, but something was changing in the town. A new-found confidence was emerging, and rather than the traditional one-way exodus of twenty-somethings leaving for other places, some were being drawn back to Luton and also attracting others.

There are so many things to draw from this story and we will explore some of them in subsequent chapters. But it is worth noting that a group of people chose to live somewhere that many of their peers would have dismissed as a bad option. How do we refuse this wisdom of the world? How do we hold true to the reality that every piece of God's earth is equally loved and significant? Those truths are chipped away at when we start to believe that some areas or towns should be avoided. For too many, 'getting involved in politics' means 'moving to London to rub shoulders with power' rather than taking the less shiny, but much more available option of serving on your own patch.

The funny thing is that if you speak to the folks involved in Gavin's church, they don't regard what has happened as anything strange or startling. They see it as a natural outflow of what church should be. They see it as a natural expression of the mission that they are called to – to be a blessing to the town of Luton. It seems to make total sense that that mission would involve the way Luton is governed and represented politically. They believe in a gospel that brings transformation to every sphere of society. To close their eyes to politics would seem irrational.

It's also worth noting that this wasn't their plan. They did not arrive with a grand scheme to change politics in Luton. As they would say, they 'just kept putting one foot in front of another', trying to follow where God was leading. Before they knew it, doors had been opened for many of them into the civic life and fabric of the town. The most important lesson to learn is the lesson of obedience.

I should note that as well as having a great impact on Luton, Gavin has also made an impressive mark at Westminster in a short space of time, with his passion, political nouse and willingness to stand up for what he believes. He has now been made a Shadow Minister for International Development.

This salt and light thing works, you know. But only if we let it.

2

BUT WHY AM I WRITING THIS?

I spent most of the early noughties singing. I was either leading worship at conferences and festivals, or I was doing the singer-songwriter thing at gigs. The only reason I ever sang was to communicate something. I am a decidedly average guitar player with a passable voice, so it wasn't musical giftedness that got me performing. During university my eyes were opened to the state of the planet through working with Tearfund on summer teams.

During one of those teams in East London, I visited council estates in Plaistow to invite folks to a barbeque at the local church. I had never been on a council estate before. I had never seen so many people living in such close proximity before.

I met a girl from Sierra Leone called Martha. She lived in a flat very different to our family home. In fact two and a half families were crowded into a space the size of our kitchen and living room. They had very few clothes and little food between them, but were the most hospitable people I had ever met – and I'm from Northern Ireland! Hearing their stories of survival in the midst of incredible poverty in their homeland awoke this white middle-class boy to the reality that how I lived my life was not how the majority of people lived their lives. My sense of gratitude for life increased exponentially and a desire to see the playing field of life levelled was firmly planted. These feelings of anger and outraged confusion began to find expression in songs, and people seemed to want to listen.

As I travelled more, the scale of inequality made me angrier. I got angry at the way that 'developing' countries were unable to trade their way out of debt because of trade rules being rigged in favour of developed countries. I was angry at our huge expenditure on weaponry and that we were selling arms to very questionable regimes. I kept on singing about it and people still seemed to want to listen. By fourth year the studies were being fitted in around the music rather than the other way round! At the end of my first year working as a doctor, I got the opportunity to work for British Youth For Christ (YFC) running their itinerant band, TVB. I loved being a doctor, but my desire to communicate in song was strong, and through a set of divine coincidences, it became abundantly clear that I should be taking a leap of faith beyond a medical career.

In the space of a week, three separate friends brought me the same job advert. I ignored the closing date, but two weeks later felt an urge to call the YFC office to find that the closing date had been extended to the very next day! I applied speedily. While still resident in Northern Ireland, I was invited to an interview in London on the only day of 1997 that I would be in London and available – three months earlier I had booked a flight to London for a conference, but taken that extra day off on the surprisingly stern advice of a colleague. When I searched the internet for information about YFC their strategy document was titled 'This is the way, walk ye in it'. Later that afternoon a nurse on my cardiology ward confided that she had been praying for me at lunchtime and that she felt the Lord had given her a verse for me. She said, 'I think it's in Isaiah – "This is the way, walk ye in it"'. I was left looking skyward going, 'Okay, I get the picture!'

So for nine years I did the music thing full time. The justice thread in my songs became stronger and stronger as I was exposed to more and more of the injustice in our world. On trips with Tearfund, Oasis and Christian Aid, we would go to visit places like Bangladesh or Uganda, and see situations in orphanages or sweatshops, then come back to raise awareness about what was going on through songs and presentations. And it was a time when NGOs were turning more of their attention to advocacy work, so as I communicated on their behalf I was starting to bump into MPs in different contexts.

As I met more and more MPs, the thing that stood out for me most was that there was simply no magic dust in Westminster. These were normal people trying to do an incredibly difficult job. It was as if the Wizard of Oz's curtain had been pulled back to reveal something less sophisticated than I had imagined. There was no great level of genius operating, from what I could see. These were not superhuman people. They had simply shown up. Parliament had been demystified for me. Having worked with some incredible surgeons, CEOs of NGOs, writers and musicians, I suddenly saw that the inhabitants of the village of Westminster were really quite ordinary. It made engaging with the place seem so much more possible.

Through those early months of interaction I also became utterly convinced of something else – that we needed a lot more Christians with spines in parliament. I had experienced so much of the creativity and brilliance of Christians working in the world of Christian organisations, and was realising that we needed more of that energy working on the inside of politics rather than merely lobbying from the outside.

What I discovered during that period is still what I share with audiences around the country today. While there is a strong theological argument about the importance of Christians being involved (see Chapters 9, 11, 12 and 13), there is also a pragmatic argument. If you look at the distribution of kingdom resources today in the UK, both in terms of people and finances, there are many more of us shouting from the outside than working on the inside of the political system. I would say the split is roughly 90% to 10%.

Of course, prophetic challenge to the parties from the outside is also vital. We need Elijahs shouting from the desert, as well as Obadiahs working in the palace.[1] Both are crucial. As Jim Wallis

---

[1] 1 Kings 18.

would say, with our campaigning we create the prophetic direction of the wind that politicians may follow.[2] But it is on the inside where the final decisions are made, and they are made by those who have shown up. Obadiah used his ministerial position of influence with Jezebel to save the lives of 100 priests, but this act would not have been possible without the preceding days and months of service to the court. So I'm not saying that party political engagement is better or more important than campaigning on single issues. It's just that we have grown up in a church culture that has encouraged one more than the other. We'll explore some of the reasons for that in the following chapters, and will see it's not surprising the numbers look the way they do.

I began to realise that I hadn't always been strategic about where I had turned up the volume. I'd been loud about dropping the debt. I'd been loud about making poverty history. I'd been loud about stopping the traffic and climate chaos. But now I was slowly learning that there's only so much you can achieve from the outside. It was fantastic to be part of Christian Aid's 'Different Drum' march calling for Hilary Benn (then Minister for International Development) to withhold money from the World Bank in protest at their harmful economic policy restrictions attached to their aid to developing countries. It happened. He did it. Amidst the cheering, what many didn't realise was that a crucial factor was Christians working on the inside at the Department for International Development (DFID) making the arguments from positions of influence.

A couple of weeks later I had an epiphany while lying in bed praying for the then Prime Minister. I realised that, conceivably, tomorrow morning the Government could sign up to every policy of my version of a Christian agenda and we would whoop excitedly. But when you look back at the issues that have defined the eras of various Prime Ministers, they are not those that are written in their manifestos. They are usually not their long-term plans, but the things that simply crop up. The key factors are, as ex-Prime Minister Harold MacMillan reputedly once put it, 'Events, dear boy, events'.

---

[2] See, for example, Jim Wallis, *God's Politics* (Lion Hudson, Oxford 2006).

They will be the reactive decisions about the next Iraq, the next Ukraine, or the next economic crisis. Surely we want people of integrity to be there on the spot, at the time, making the decisions that will have long-term effects on our nation and the rest of the world. Just having the right policy slate and promoting it from outside the system will never achieve that. Surely we want people who will stop for a moment and consult ancient deeper wisdom, rather than just opinion polls, focus groups or Twitter feeds. Surely we want folks who might just pray about the wisest course of action when confronted with terrorist attacks, wars, climate catastrophes, viral outbreaks or domestic rioting. Campaigning from the outside will never be enough. And the most far-sighted policy can never be enough. Showing up ourselves is what just might help.

So having met some of the MPs, I was invited to help with some of the prayer and worship that happens around Westminster. Through this I got to know many more of the Christians who were seeking to demonstrate the kingdom there. Because of my passion to see the global economic system rewired, I was asked to write some articles for *The Common Good* – the magazine of what was then called the Christian Socialist Movement. After a while I was asked to edit the magazine, and then join the executive. A while later, the Director of CSM moved on to a new job, and quite a few people said, 'Flan, you should do that'. I had spent most of my life strenuously avoiding any responsibility to leave space for creativity, so I baulked at the idea. It became clear, however, that a door was opening that I should walk through. On the day I was appointed, the Chairman Alun Michael rang me to say, 'We had three excellent candidates who could all do the job, but one was safe, one was risky and one was dangerous.' He made it clear I was the latter!

The last six years have been an immense privilege. There have been so many amazing and frustrating moments, but by far the most exciting aspect has been our future candidates programme. They are a bunch of phenomenal twenty- and thirty-somethings who we have been supporting in their desire to stand as candidates. They are making a conscious and costly decision to show up.

Many of these folks have been youth workers, community workers and social workers. Some of them have intentionally moved onto tough housing estates. When they speak about communities, their passion for real people shines through. Poverty is not just a concept to them. When current MPs meet them and hear their stories, they are blown away. More than one has turned to me after a session and said, 'These are the sort of MPs we need in the future'. Some have already been selected for the 2015 general election or for local council seats, and I believe many more will be selected in 2020 and beyond. This is a long-term strategy.

Our mantra has been the famous African proverb – 'If you want to go fast, go it alone, but if you want to go far, go together'. We will do this not as individuals but as a body. That may mean that things happen more slowly, but that is alright. We must come without the selfish ambition, and power-hungry self-promotion that exists in the political world but intentionally adopting the opposite spirit.

The future candidates have therefore been getting to know each other, praying together, and holding each other accountable. We wanted to foster an atmosphere where they could reflect theologically on different policy issues in a safe environment. They are getting media training and opportunities to call on the policy expertise of various Christian agencies to help develop their political outlook.

They have been working hard for each other while seeking selection and campaigning for each other once they are selected for a seat. The selection process involves an awful lot of phone calls and door knocking to convince local party members that you should be their candidate, so the camaraderie has been vital.

The Conservative Christian Fellowship has a similar, slightly more developed leadership programme called IMPACT. Participants spend a series of weekends and day seminars exploring various topics including: The Bible and Politics; policies that changed the world; transformational leadership; justice and ethics. This has already produced quite a few Members of Parliament. The Liberal Democrat Christian Forum also encourages prospective candidates by offering advice, prayer support, and connecting them with mentors.

Which party?

As I reflect on my own journey, for me, the biggest stalling factor was deciding which political party to join. There is something about pinning your colours to the mast that makes you feel vulnerable. This was especially difficult because I can be an outrageous procrastinator. When you add to that my Northern Irish upbringing, where political parties were mostly about a border rather than other policies, you can see why I was a slow learner. For years I sat on the fence wondering whether I was X or whether I was Y. Certain policies turned me towards certain parties and then others would put me off, returning me to studied fence-sitting. I analysed manifestos online. I read every piece of literature that came through my door. Yes I am that sad. I knew that my passion for economic justice had me veering to the left, but interestingly for me, there wasn't a decisive policy-based moment when I knew which party I should choose. It was actually about people.

We follow a relational God. I truly believe your journey into a political party may be as much about the relational links you are presented with as your commitment to all their policies. At the end of the day, the statistics show that Christians have a leaning to one party or another because of their cultural background more than any particular policy beliefs. If I had been brought up in Torquay, who knows which party I would be in! I would say I had the confidence to finally sign on the line because some full-on Christians who I deeply respected were already members, and it seemed like they hadn't yet been 'eaten up by the beast', or, for sci-fi fans, 'assimilated into the Borg'.

Another problem that people come up against when thinking about which party to join is the fact that they live in a very safe seat. So, for example, their political sympathies lie with the Conservative party, but they live in an area that has always been deep red. I understand the frustration. Where there is a safe seat scenario, there are much less likely to be living, breathing groups representing the other parties. But there will always be at least a few people there.

Here is where we have to shout loud and clear that it is not all about Westminster. One thing to remember is that even if across a whole constituency, the voting is weighted strongly one way or the other, it will vary greatly in individual wards. Wards are the subdivisions of boroughs that elect local or county councillors. Because these are much smaller (with sometimes just a few thousand voters) they may not reflect the demographics of the constituency as a whole. That means there may well be life in party groupings operating in these areas.

It's also worth noting that being involved in politics isn't all about winning. In some of these safe seat areas it is all the more important – and actually sometimes even more possible, because of the small numbers of people involved – to be making a different case in the public debate. Many of our members stand for parliament or council and lose with great regularity. They are not strange masochists, but people who know that it is important that their voice is heard. Whether they get elected or not, these elections provide them with incredible opportunities to speak up for those who cannot speak for themselves.

My standard playful line when I speak to audiences about choosing a party is that I don't care which horse you get on, just get on one. And it's 80% true! I'd prefer you were in the horse race rather than just watching it.

So you can see that my story of getting involved, like Gavin's, wasn't one of a grand Damascene call, but just putting one foot in front of the other, allowing God to join the dots and make the connections. That's now what I try to do for others. I would love to say I am some grand pioneer, but I'm not sure I can. I am almost radical. Whether it was coming to parliament, getting involved in the prayer group, visiting an MP's surgery, or the party issue, it needed conversations with other believers who were already there. These people invite us out into the deeper water. They are standing there like Anthony Gormley's famous statues, extending a hand to give us the confidence we need to step away from our comfort zones. There is a long line of them, each making a separate invitation, that eventually leads us to where we are not just wading, but swimming. Out in the depths, we will be subject to the waves that will come crashing in, but that is where we will feel alive. The depths are where we will need help and prayer from others, and our own prayer lives and discipleship will probably take a step in the right direction too.

Not neutral

In the past, Christian organisations have produced books about politics that have rightly bent over backwards to include voices from every point on the spectrum. They have been incredibly helpful in giving a bird's-eye view of the subject. This sometimes gives the impression that the church has an arms length approach to politics, fostered partly by leaders who understandably want to appear neutral, but thereby dislocate their people from any ability or vocabulary to engage. But even if leaders do decide to stay neutral (though increasingly many don't), it should never be a neutrality based on silence.

What you are reading now is more of a personal journey. Also, I don't want readers to think that they will only ever hover above politics rather than get involved. So rather than be intentionally vague with warm, fuzzy words I will be up front about where I am coming from.

Along with my dear friends and colleagues Colin Bloom (Conservative Christian Fellowship) and Claire Mathys (Liberal Democrat Christian Forum), I run Christians in Politics. I am also the Director of Christians on the Left. It's important that the three of us run Christians in Politics rather than someone neutral. That way we can model what it is that we are calling people to. When we go to speak at churches, events and festivals, we can answer the questions and concerns people have accurately because we do actually inhabit those worlds. The three of us have strongly held reasons for being members of our three parties. But what seems to surprise people is that we have an even more strongly-held belief that our primary allegiance is not to a party or an ideology but to the King of Kings. We stand together and proclaim that kingdom comes before tribe.

So this book is not written by someone who is neutral. It is written by me – a living, breathing, Bible-believing Jesus-following member of the Labour party. But while I am not neutral, and shouldn't pretend to be, my co-directors and I all desperately desire an influx of Christians into the Conservative party, the Liberal Democrat party and all the other parties. That's why we actually work together quite effectively. It's because we want the same thing – to see kingdom values at the heart of local and national government. We all know that our parties, and thereby the country, will be better for an influx of believers – those who hold kingdom before tribe – into politics. That doesn't always make us popular with our own tribes, but hey, that's not what we're here for. In fact the work of Christians in Politics has grown exponentially since people have started to realise that we are serious about this. So what you read here represents our shared narrative, but we thought it should come from just one voice.

Christians in politics

Some people can't believe that we have managed to form a functional organisation with brothers and sisters from the other main political parties. They assume, from the media, that we never talk to one another. The reality is that there is much more co-operation going on in the House of Commons than the thirty ridiculous minutes of Prime Minister's Questions would have you believe.

Christians in Politics is not, however, focused on Westminster. That is the job of Christians in Parliament. We are focused on the rest of the UK. Our mission is to inspire and equip Christians to get involved in party politics. So, through speaking at various churches, events and festivals, or writing for various media outlets, we try to tell the story of what God is already doing in the world of politics and invite others to join in. We have a team of speakers who will happily come to an event near you, so just give us a call or drop us an email.

It's important to note that this isn't just about the three most established parties – there are also Christians involved with SNP, Plaid Cymru, Green, UKIP and the Northern Irish parties. Where there are Christians that share the 'kingdom first' narrative, we are reaching out to them – the relationships are building as we speak. We are certainly not the whole deal. It's just that we're here. There are of course also many believers who consciously choose to be politically active outside the constraints of traditional party politics. I am a cheerleader for these folks too. There are independent candidates who I admire greatly. There are others with whom I walk on protest marches, whose views I share on the need for systemic change which politics in its current form cannot fully deliver. It's just one part of the picture.

So I will be including plenty of stories from others, but the bulk of this is me. That way you can have an actual human to connect with as you read rather than a faceless entity. So you can agree with me, or scream at me, but at least you can get into a dialogue with someone who exists!

If you are starting to feel a nudge towards to this stuff, try to think about who you could talk to. Are there people who have already taken some of these steps? If you feel like you don't know anyone, then as Christians in Politics we will be more than happy to connect you up with any number of people who would love to chat. Just email us via the website – www.christiansinpolitics.org. uk or participate in the discussion forum. Please log on and join in as you read.

Here's an example of someone who took these steps.

Bukky Olawoyin

Bukky is a Conservative councillor in Hatfield and a deacon at Jesus House for All Nations Church. Born in Bolton, he spent most of his childhood in Nigeria.

'There was a period in 2006–07 when the newspapers were full of comment that there weren't enough black role models in the community. Around the same time, a comment was made about how much foreigners take [from society] but don't contribute. I asked some friends, 'In the last few years, how many of us have given to charities (apart from churches) and how many of us have got involved in the community?' Having thrown down the gauntlet, I decided to become a governor at my daughter's school. I enjoyed it so much I began tweeting about it and putting things on Facebook, making people aware of what was happening.

The myth is that the Conservatives are typically a middle class, white party and they don't have any time for non-whites. But I went along to a meeting to find out what it was all about. After I joined the party and began volunteering, I'd discuss things with friends and give feedback to the party, so that their views were represented.

If Jesus were on the earth today, he would be involved in public life. He teaches us to be a blessing to whoever we come into contact with, and the Bible encourages us to be valuable tools and help others. Being a councillor helps me to empathise with people; it allows me to be bothered about them.'

Follow Bukky *@bukkyolawoyin*

3

BUT I DON'T CARE ABOUT POLITICS

'That's all very well for Luton and all very well for you. That's just one place, and that's just your story', you may say. Fair enough. I also hear this:

> I don't care about politics. I'm not interested in politics. Those politicians – they're all the same. They haven't a clue about what's going on out here in the real world. Politics does nothing for me. Why should I give them my vote? They don't care about me.

I have heard these sorts of statements regularly over the last ten years. And I have some sympathy for this view. Given what we pick up about politics from the media, I don't blame people. But when somebody says, 'I don't care about politics' I have to ask the question in return, 'But do you care about your neighbourhood?' To be honest, if your answer to that question is no, then you are probably holding the wrong book in your hand. I won't have the space in this book to convince you that your neighbours or your neighbourhood may be worth caring about. Grab your remote control, lie back on the sofa and enjoy your life.

But if your answer to that question is 'Yes,' then let me put it to you that you do care about politics. You perhaps just don't know it yet.

Jesus said, 'Love your neighbour as yourself' (Mark 12:31). So we need to love others in the way that we love ourselves. But how do we love ourselves? We love ourselves through a huge variety of mental, physical and spiritual attitudes and practices that keep the show of life on the road. We feed ourselves. We buy clothes for ourselves. We communicate with others. We establish our official place in society through things like NHS registration and National Insurance numbers. We find jobs and somewhere to live. We organise diaries. We find love. We connect with God. It is worth stopping to remember that for some people, even people in our neighbourhood, these basic things may not be true.

Loving our neighbour 'as ourselves' must therefore mean caring about all these aspects of other peoples' lives too. It doesn't get much more complicated than that. Our efforts to sort our lives out are not solely spiritual, so why should we shrink our efforts for others to that arena? I genuinely used to hear church leaders say, 'The government is there to cover the practical. I'll just cover the spiritual'. This dualistic theology has sadly had a long-term impact on our thinking and practice. Happily things are changing, but the legacy still lurks. It led the church to build a separate subculture, leaving 'politics to the politicians' as if they were a different breed of human, limiting our influence on society. The church's voice seemed to be based on old privilege rather than our present engagement. We regret that now!

You simply cannot divorce the personal from the social, economic, cultural and political environments within which we live and move and have our being. They have a huge influence on us, and to address personal needs without addressing the context in which a life sits makes little sense and can actually lead to a lot of frustration.

There is a 78-year-old lady on our block called Marie. The life she lives is similar to that of many other older people all over the UK. Visualise an elderly person who you know well and ask yourself these questions, inserting your friend's name.

Do you care that Marie's bins are collected? Do you care that her local hospital is well supplied with the drugs she needs? Do you care that her bedroom is damp? Do you care that a GP can see her in her home? Do you care that she is safe from the scam artists who would attempt to snatch her hard-fought-for savings? Do you care about her noisy neighbours? Do you care about her ability to use public transport?

If you care about even one of these things, you care about politics. You care about politics because you care about people.

Mick Duncan from the charity Urban Neighbours of Hope, who lived for twelve years in a slum in Manila with his family, explains it like this. He spoke about one of his neighbours for whom simply being a friend meant being involved in her life on many levels. She was in extreme poverty, so there were times when he simply needed to share meals with her, or give gifts of cash and items that would help her survive. He was fighting on a *practical front*. She was also heavily involved in some of the occult practices that ensnare many in the Philippines, so Mick had to fight on a *spiritual front*. There was much prayer. The land on which they lived was not acknowledged as 'real' by the government, so she was not an official citizen, with all the benefits like healthcare and education which that would bring. It also meant that the area did not receive proper sanitation or refuse systems. So Mick had to fight for her on a *political front* for the land and for all of her neighbours to be recognised. The point must be made in the midst of all of this that she was also blessing him, and he was learning huge amounts from her. But you can see that to focus on any one of these areas to the detriment of the other would avoid being the neighbour that she needed.

As human beings, we are not islands. We are affected by our family history. We are influenced by our peers. We are impacted by the laws of the land in which we live. The more you love people, the more you see how their internal wiring is profoundly affected by their circumstances and vice versa. This is a two-way street. To attempt to bless someone by simply focusing on their beliefs and thinking means that any progress made may be reversed by their circumstances. To attempt to bless someone by simply focusing on their circumstances means that any positive change may be short-lived because of an unhealthy view of themselves. The more you love people, the more you want to see every aspect of their lives transformed. If you only love them enough to see their spiritual lives sorted out, then your love runs the danger of being a cover for increasing the size of your church.

That is why it simply isn't an option for us to opt out of political activity, leaving it to someone else. It may not take up the majority of our time, but we need to realise that there is a political aspect to our lives and the lives of our neighbours. We all live in a certain area of a certain town in a certain country. Who we are is hugely influenced by the laws of that society at local and national level. We cannot avoid their influence.

The very mention of the word politics may have already had you setting this book down and heading for the kettle, but please wait for a second and let me deconstruct what it actually means.

Our word politics stems from the Greek *polis*, which referred to their ancient city states, but also more widely to the idea of citizenship and the actual body of citizens. Politics, from the Greek *politikos*, literally 'of, for, or relating to citizens' is simply the practice and theory of influencing other people on an individual, civic or global level. So each of us practises politics every day as we subtly (or sometimes unsubtly) influence one another in conversation, in the playground, in the pub or in the living room. To say that we are not into politics is to misrepresent the word. The truth is that we are all into politics but sometimes only up to a certain arbitrary line which we have drawn somewhere between the individual and civic levels of involvement.

Politics simply describes how we order society and people. And as we will see in Chapter 12, throughout Scripture, God shows that he is particularly passionate about how we organise ourselves as a society. We know he cares about the state of our hearts, but he also cares about the heart of our state.

Culture shaping

Here are a few relatively recent examples that illustrate how much politics shapes the culture we inhabit. In the big scheme of things, these may seem like small examples, but they illustrate that even small decisions have a profound impact on our lives.

Seatbelt legislation

Seatbelts existed before you had to wear them. Some people did but most people didn't. When the legislation was proposed there was a loud debate between safety campaigners and those who believed their rights were being infringed.

The funny thing is that they were. That's what laws do. They infringe our 'rights'. For the sake of the common good they establish some norms in society that inevitably curb our freedoms. Speed limits are another great example.

This is why I get hugely frustrated when I hear Christians say that we shouldn't be imposing our opinions on others. Yes, we must be gracious in our speech, aware of the church's complicity in past unhelpful coercion, but coercion is partly what politics is about. That is what law is about. Someone has to make some judgment calls to help create order. And it will never be a popular job. You may try to do what is best in the interests of the nation as a whole, but you will inevitably annoy some people, because one person's rights will always interfere with someone else's rights. My neighbour's right to play their music loudly at 2 am infringes on my right to a decent night's sleep. Here is where a society that has slidden into individualism can be very dangerous. Politicians may just horse-trade between competing rights and whoever shouts the loudest for their rights wins. It's not a healthy way to make law, or run a society. Life should be as much about responsibilities to one another as it is about individual rights. So it's not easy to be the ones having to decide these things, but if we don't do it, someone else will, and we may end up grumbling an awful lot.

So seatbelt legislation arrived, and it changed our culture. It slowly changed our habits. All it took was the odd story from the friend of a friend who had been stopped by the police to convince us that we had probably better wear them. And not many years later we don't think twice about wearing them. Has it resulted in fewer road deaths? Yes. Has it infringed our freedoms? Yes. The job of the lawmaker is often to balance the common good with personal freedoms, but the mistake is to pretend that this is not what is going on! Our decision-making (which is something internal) can be changed for better or worse by laws (which are external). So whether we as Christians articulate our primary passion more in terms of seeing individual lives changed, or in terms of seeing the nation at large transformed, politics hugely influences both.

Smoking in workplaces

Hilariously it was the Irish government, of all nations, who first pursued legislation to outlaw smoking in workplaces. Again two conflicting rights were grinding up against one another. My right to smoke wherever I want and your right to not inhale my smoke. Again many claimed the law would be unworkable. People claimed it would be the end for pubs and restaurants. But the law changed, and now many can't even remember how it used to be. Legislation changes culture, either for better or worse (though I believe both the seatbelt and smoking examples have changed it for the better). People's behaviour has changed because what is deemed to be acceptable in culture has changed.

You can see that the law not only draws lines in the sand, it affects the contours of the whole beach. That is why some of the discussion around issues like marriage and banking often misses the point. People argue we should have no comment to make on things that don't affect us or that we shouldn't impose our views on others.But over time laws do create new norms. You may agree or disagree with those new norms, but surely you cannot argue that they only have an effect in law, and not in public consciousness. So we need to have an active rather than a passive engagement with legislation and its impact on individual lives. No woman or man is an island.

Organisation

I rather suspect that, if you were to abolish politics, a few years later something looking suspiciously like politics would reappear. To prevent chaos we simply need to organise ourselves, and establish some basic norms to allow communities to function. As Christians we should be hugely excited about the idea of institutions and structures that prevent lawlessness. Without these structures in place, mob rule rules. The powerful and the wealthy use their financial and military might to get their way. Sadly this is still the case in many parts of the world. And without governance, it is the poor who suffer the most. They have no private army to support their cause or offshore bank accounts for a rainy day. In short, people get trampled, and we should celebrate the fact that we have institutions to make and keep the law. But in our fallenness, those who enforce the law can exploit people intentionally or unintentionally just as much as the masked raider. That's why we should be even more thankful that we have the privilege of voting for those who will run these institutions. Many in our world still do not have that safeguard. Hopefully you are also starting to see that you could be not just someone who votes, but one of the people running the institutions.

We all do politics – we just don't call it politics. We organise committees to help run things like village fêtes. Politics is just one oversized, complicated village fête committee. It should be noted of course that the politics of a village fête committee can be pretty shocking too! We set up committees to run church services, or mission projects. We form building committees. As humans we organise ourselves. To avoid 'politics' by drawing a strange line in the sand that says we will organise locally or within the walls of the church, but not engage with the way things are organised on a civic or national level makes little intellectual or practical sense.

Hopefully the church is emerging from the false secular/sacred mentality that left us as bystanders. The trouble is we are also citizens trapped in the present day and therefore another storm is breaking on our shore.

The consumerisation of life and politics

It's hardly an original observation to say that in the twenty-first century the citizens of planet earth are becoming increasingly house-trained as consumers. Every time we raise our heads and protest that we are more than economic units, powerful vested interests put us back in our flat-pack boxes. The observation has been applied to many spheres of life – whether it is the 'drive-in-bless-me' model of church, the increasing sense of entitlement in young people, or our attitudes to sport (more watching, less playing). A point less often articulated is the impact that consumerism has had on politics and public service.

A society that used to revolve around church congregations, parish councils, unions, guilds and other planks of civic society has become increasingly atomised. In those bodies people understood the need to give something to society as well as take from it. Increasingly the attitude of many to politics is 'what are they going to do for me?', as opposed to 'how can I make my voice heard?' or 'how can I play my part?' A friend was recently flabbergasted when he asked the gent sitting next to him on a flight what he did for a living. 'I try to destroy the idea of family and community,' he said. It turned out he was a senior marketing executive, and in a sleep-deprived state had let slip a moment of candid honesty. He went on to explain that once you make people believe they are autonomous units without wider reference points, you can sell them almost anything. 'So much easier to pick off,' he said. It is shocking to hear, but it rings painfully true. If our status comes through acquisition rather than relationships, we are logically and powerfully drawn to shop. The same applies in our attitudes to politics. Increasingly, we merely tick a box every four or five years to register whether we like the current product or not.

As Christians this is surely not an option. We follow the one who seeks to give, give some more and then keep on giving. We are called to emulate him rather become selfish receptacles. So why in the realm of politics does the church so often cast itself in the role of consumer and commentator, rather than participant?

In the same way that we have got used to switching energy providers for a better deal, we import that attitude into politics. Who will give us the best deal? We choose our mobile network provider and we select our government provider of choice. Before we choose we reflect on how badly they have let us down before and how long we were on hold with their customer services. Have they answered our concerns? Are they going to get cheaper or more expensive? Who will make us feel better? And how we feel is key. Mobile phone networks and political parties don't spend money on advertising for fun. They know it works. They make us feel good about the product we are buying. And that is the point. We are not just consumers, but we have been fooled into believing we are. It also suits some involved in politics to keep us as consumers. We are more controllable and subdued. We are less likely to rise up in revolt if we are happily entertained. So our entertainment is encouraged. *The Hunger Games* caught our imagination because it isn't so far from the truth. The sad thing is that for many of us politics has become simply a middle-class soap opera, allowing some sense of intellectual superiority as we discuss it. It frustrates me that even church leaders fall into this trap. As Christians in Politics we meet lots of them, and when we start discussions it is disappointing to hear that so many of their questions are about the soap opera of Westminster rather than the political realities of their communities.

The London riots of 2011 exposed some painful truths. No longer were the young rising up because they wanted better hospitals, less war in their name, or more jobs. Apart from the initial frustration in response to Mark Duggan's shooting, the folks near me were mostly rioting for better trainers and mobile phones. On the second night of the riots I was strategically walking one block away from the Walworth Road (our local high street), and I bumped into three sets of young people running with huge flat screen TVs in shopping trolleys. I had to stop and blink. Here risks were not being taken for the greater good of a country, community or family. Here risks were being taken to view Wayne Rooney scoring goals in high definition or to allow the destruction of alien worlds with XBOX surround sound.

We are not immune to this growing consumerisation in the church. In fact sometimes it helps us keep our noses clean if we remain as consumers of the government 'product' rather than believe we could be participants. One example of how this plays out happens just before every election.

Of the hustings that took place before the last general election, 67% were organised by churches. Others were not organised by churches but took place in their buildings. This is a good thing. Hustings are an important part of the political process, enabling local people to size up those who would like to be their future MP. But I wonder if, in all the energy that is spent resourcing churches to run hustings, are we missing something? I am all in favour of Christian agencies providing briefings to help church members get their heads around the issues before the event. It is an important part of political education. My problem with our eggs all being in this particular basket is that the church is yet again cast in the role of onlooker and commentator. We feel that we will have done our Christian and civic duty if we asked a good question and got a sense of who we will vote for. In fact if you analysed most of the output from Christian media outlets in the run up to an election, most of their content seems to be 'Information to help you decide which party or which candidate is most Christian'. These are not unimportant questions, but again we are left as critiquers and commentators rather than participants.

That's why in the run-up to the 2015 election, Christians in Politics in partnership with the Evangelical Alliance and an array of other organisations, are running a campaign called *Show Up*. Any similarity to book titles living or dead is purely coincidental!

We want to shift some of the energy away from commentary to participation. Both are important, but at the moment there are bucket loads of the former going on and not so much of the latter. We want to challenge folks that the next time the hustings come around in 2020 that they could be the ones answering the questions rather than just asking them. Which I think you will agree is probably more difficult, but Jesus didn't call us to take up our matchsticks and follow him.

One way Christians are making the journey from commentary to participation is through community organising. It has also been hugely influential in shifting people's perceptions of what politics actually is. The local church has been waking up to the importance of being political, realising that power is not something just held by politicians or heads of corporations. Communities themselves have inherent power. It just needs to be channelled effectively. Here I've asked David Barclay (from the Centre for Theology and Community) to explain a little bit more:

> Community organising involves building an alliance of religious congregations, schools and other civic associations to work together on issues of common concern. It seeks to build a 'relational culture': encouraging people to share their stories through one-to-one conversations and then to come together and identify ways in which their areas can be changed for the better. When people with common concerns are in relationship, they are in a position to challenge those with power to deliver change (be that environmental improvements, better pay for workers, or improved public services). The home of community organising in the UK is an organisation called Citizens UK. While their campaigns are on specific, winnable issues, the wider goal is to build a local and national alliance with an ongoing set of relationships of trust and commitment – where each successful campaign not only brings a tangible result but develops grassroots leadership and the power of people in Britain's poorest neighbourhoods to work together for the common good.
>
> The Living Wage Campaign is the most famous example of Citizens UK's work. It was launched in the mid-1990s after a listening campaign in East London. Elders in local churches and mosques felt that an increasing gap was developing between the generations, with a lack in mutual comprehension and respect. No one imagined a community organising campaign could solve such a huge and long-term issue. However, it was felt that low pay was exacerbating the problem. Parents on low wages were being forced to choose between having enough time for their children and earning enough money for them. Hence, the Living Wage Campaign – the movement promoting an hourly rate of pay that would free East Londoners from such an invidious choice.
>
> Local people not only chose the issue on which to act. They also won the victories. Early in the Living Wage Campaign, the

HSBC tower in Canary Wharf was selected as a 'target'. Leaders of the religious and civic groups in the London Citizens (the local arm of Citizens UK) wrote to the management of the bank. The moral case they presented was compelling. The regeneration of the Docklands was supposed to have been about improving the life-chances of East Londoners.

Ten years on, employers who don't pay the living wage are now the exception in Canary Wharf. The London living wage has been championed by Ken Livingstone and Boris Johnson in their terms as Mayor, and a research unit at City Hall calculates the figure annually. Hard-nosed multinationals now speak of a 'Business Case for the Living Wage', because of the increases in staff retention and productivity which flow from decent pay.

Many who have dipped their toes into community organising are now also joining political parties as they discover that change is possible.

In summary, I hope that you are starting to believe that you do care about politics because you do care about your neighbourhood and nation, and I hope that we are all on the journey from consumers to participants.

4

SHOWING UP: SCOTLAND

Showing up: in the referendum

If you want to know what showing up looks like you don't have to look far. Because there's one population, one piece of the UK, in the very corner of Europe, that's bucking the trend of disengagement happening right across Europe.

I give you Scotland.

In 2014, if you were under a rock somewhere, you might have missed the referendum on Scottish Independence. Whatever your views or the outcome of the vote this was an exercise in democracy unprecedented in modern times. When polling day came 84.59% of the population showed up to vote. That's right 85%. Figures that political geeks like me can only dream off. Not only that but 16- and 17-year-olds could show up in this vote and show up they did. Young people debating politics in schools up and down the country, building sites, pubs, toddler groups all resounding to the common question ... 'What way are you thinking?' Politics for the masses in every corner of a nation. As I say, the stuff political dreams are made of.

And boy, did the church show up. Debates up and down the country, national prayer days, a voice in the debate. The Evangelical Alliance asked the best question of the whole referendum: *What Kind of Nation?* What kind of nation should Scotland actually be? Christians wrestled with how to build a better nation, with questions of identity and vision, hope and justice, questions that are timeless, aspirations that are achievable, if only we will continue to show up.

Showing up at Holyrood

Showing up can also be the quiet things, the faithful things, week after week when no one is watching. In Holyrood there is a team of ladies (and a few men) who, every week, show up.

It started in 1998, when at the National Prayer Breakfast in Scotland, the host Lord Mackay of Clashfern, addressed the Breakfast: 'The word is there will be either no prayer or only multi-faith prayer in the new Scottish Parliament.'

These words struck Anne McIntyre at the time, and were to affect her life for the next 16 years. She felt very strongly that this could have a deeply negative effect on the nation.

In 1999 when the Scottish Parliament reconvened after almost 300 years, the first debate and decision taken was to *not* pray for parliament or God's blessing upon their work. In Westminster business starts every day with Christian prayer. Holyrood voted to have just a four-minute 'Time for Reflection' at 2 pm every Tuesday, to start the weekly Chamber business. This is led mostly by Christian ministers, based on proportional representation, but also by those of other faiths and none.

CARE asked Anne to lead a campaign with them for Christian prayer. Thousands wrote in – the largest postbag the Parliament had for many years – but that battle was lost.

So that first year she went to each of the eight regions of Scotland, meeting with intercessors until each of the 129 MSPs were 'adopted' to be prayed for each day for the first four years. At the beginning of the next Parliamentary year, she was given the Board Room of the Free Church of Scotland to meet to pray weekly, just two minutes from the first temporary meeting place of the Parliament. Her desire was to actually go into the Parliament and pray during the 'Time for Reflection'.

Gradually God has stirred hearts and brought others, and today members come from all over Scotland, some travelling two or three hours. There are about 45 committed to pray and usually about 20 meeting and going down to the Parliament, as they have been each week now for fourteen years. In the morning they meet to worship and pray in the Salvation Army, a ten-minute walk from Holyrood, and then go down to the Parliament for the time of reflection, and stay most of the afternoon. They speak with and get to know many members of staff during this time.

These ladies are completely apolitical, yet they faithfully pray every Tuesday, outside and inside Holyrood. Sitting in the gallery in their distinctive red jackets, they have become know as 'the thin red line', a reference to the Argyll and Sutherland Highlanders who defended the stocks of the British Army in the battle of Balaclava in the Crimean War, and indicating their willingness to defend their faith.

The team prays for leaders, for all the MSPs, regardless of politics or faith, and for all the staff of Parliament. Anyone can contact them with confidential prayer needs and they can offer support and prayer. Many MSPs have registered their deep appreciation for this. They are a group of amazing ladies who simply choose to *show up*.

Dave Thompson

Dave Thompson is the MSP for Skye, Lochaber and Badenoch.

Dave was christened in St Gerardine's Church of Scotland, Lossiemouth, and went to Sunday school until he was fourteen, when he discovered the world and more or less forgot about Jesus. Fortunately, as he confessed to me, the Lord didn't forget about him and, thirty years later in 1993, he and his wife, Veronica started to attend Kinmylies Baptist Church, Inverness.

Dave eventually accepted Jesus as a personal Saviour and was baptised, along with Veronica, on the 21 April 2002 and hasn't looked back since. He is now back in the Church of Scotland at Kinmylies Parish Church, Inverness.

Dave inherited an interest in politics from his father, who was an active Trades Unionist in Morayshire, which was a very Conservative area. Lossiemouth was also the birthplace of Ramsay MacDonald, Britain's first Labour Prime Minister and Dave was born just across the road from the house he built for his mother. Dave's family knew him well and all this added to the political mix.

Dave has always had a sense of social justice and for standing up for what is right. He led a walkout of boys who worked in a local fish factory after school when he was fourteen, following a dispute over pay. He joined the Scalemakers' Union when he started work just before his sixteenth birthday and also joined the SNP in Elgin a few months later. He was a founder member of the Lossiemouth branch of the SNP the year after, in 1966. Dave spent 34 years in Local Government, ending up as Director of Protective Services for Highland Council, which he left at the end of 2001.

Dave first stood for the Scottish Parliament in 2003, for the Ross, Skye and Inverness West seat, and was also on the SNP's list for the Highlands and Islands Regional seat. He failed on both counts. In 2005 he then stood for the Inverness, Nairn, Badenoch and Strathspey Westminster seat and failed again.

Then, in 2007, Dave stood again for Ross, Skye and Inverness West, where he failed once more, but got elected for the Highlands and Islands Regional list seat. He was the very last MSP to be elected, and only after a recount, which he forced, after challenging the Returning Officer. It turned out the officer had made a mistake. His seat gave the SNP 47 seats, just one more than Labour, and put them into government for the first time ever, but as a minority.

At the last election, in 2011, Dave won the revised boundary seat of Skye, Lochaber and Badenoch with an increased majority and is now a member of a majority SNP government.

I will let Dave explain the place his faith takes in his politics in his own words:

'I have changed a lot on my journey with Christ and but still have a long way to go.

As a Christian I believe we should be salt and light in the world and that God put me into politics and that we should not isolate ourselves from worldly matters. In doing so he gave me good guidance in 2 Corinthians 6:17 where he says 'Be ye separate'. Spurgeon interpreted it like this 'You should be separate from the world in your actions, if a thing be right though you lose by it, it must be done. If it be wrong, though you would gain by it, you must scorn the sin for your master's sake.'

In my nearly eight years as an MSP I have always been open and upfront about my faith and have often spoken in debates where I highlight the fact. I am active in sponsoring the group, Scotland United in Prayer for Parliament (SUPP) and attend the monthly Parliamentary Prayer breakfasts. I am also a member of the Scottish Bible Society and a Trustee of the National Prayer Breakfast Scotland. I also helped found Christians for Independence (CFI) in 2009, which is a cross-party group promoting God's word in politics and, of course, independence.

Most politicians will tell you that faith is a private matter but I believe that, as my views are coloured by my Christian beliefs, as other's are coloured by their particular beliefs, they can't remain private.

There are many issues raised in Parliament, like assisted suicide, gay marriage, abortion, stem cell research, poverty, nuclear weapons, slavery, prostitution, poor housing, fair trade, asylum seekers, immigration, war, gambling and the environment, to name but a few. The Bible has much to say about these issues but any politician who goes into a debate just quoting Scripture, which is often misunderstood and misused, is foolish to say the least. The point is that all of God's values are eminently suited to good logical arguments and we must marshal these to win our case.

The problem for a politician who is a Christian, however, is that you must overcome the perception that you are biased and bigoted from the start. To do this, more of us have to put our heads above the parapet and enter politics. I can, of course, sympathise with Christians who are already in politics but who keep their faith to themselves – but wonder what Jesus would say?'

5

BUT IT'S A DIRTY GAME, ISN'T IT

The only thing necessary for the triumph of evil, is for good men to do nothing.

Edmund Burke

For the Christian, to mix religion and politics is not an option; it is an obligation.

George Austin, former Archbishop of York

By now you may be convinced that politics is important, or you may have skipped to this chapter because you already were. But there is another problem.

Can we speak candidly? Since there are just the two of us here. You and me. Reader and writer. Let's not ignore the enormous elephant in the room. (Okay, so there are three of us.) People may agree that politics is important, but people just don't like politics. Or perhaps people don't like politicians. You don't need to tell me. I hear it all the time. It would be silly of me to write a book about politics and pretend that is not the case.

The irony is that the brand 'Politics' is more in need of good PR than possibly any other brand, yet there are more PR experts involved in it than most other fields.

To convince someone of the positive potential of politics in the early twenty-first century is a bit like trying to convince someone of the benefits of flossing your teeth. At a certain level we understand it to be true, but there is a big difference between that and doing anything about it. Those little bits of thread are very awkward to pull off the reel, and then it's difficult to get your fingers in the right place, and then there's the blood. It's all strangely similar to the political journey. Most people don't know where to start. But it is that gap (to continue the flossing analogy) between knowing it's important and doing anything about it which I hope that this book will help you bridge, both conceptually and practically.

So before anyone tries to make a case, some deconstruction is necessary. To be more specific, through my work with Christians in Politics over the last few years I have heard many people quote many reasons why Christians don't get involved in party politics. In fact at our Christians in Politics workshops we regularly ask church leaders and other attendees to brainstorm a list. The list always seems to be longest when we attend theological colleges! I think the record is twenty-eight reasons why Christians generally don't get involved. Sometimes they are legitimate concerns, but too often they reveal our skewed priorities or misconceptions. Five of these reasons stand out far above the others because of the regularity with which they are reported, so I thought it would be a useful exercise to look at each of them in turn in their own chapter. And the first is this:

It's a dirty game, they're all on the make, and they can't be trusted

In recent years, this has become an understandable response. No one should be trying to defend the ridiculous excesses exposed during the expenses scandal that broke in 2009, and I have no intention of doing so here. A *laissez-faire* culture was allowed to develop that ignored the need for those who serve the public to abide by the same standards expected of the public.

But we must keep our ears open to all sides of the story. Our media have a vested interest in serving up what is tragic and scandalous, at the expense of the honourable and mundane. And sadly it would appear that we have similar appetites. Our 'build them up, then knock them down' celebrity culture applies just as much to politics as it does to sport and music. While focussing on the number of MPs who grossly betrayed people's trust – perhaps about thirty – we didn't often hear that there were approximately 620 still working hard to do an incredibly difficult job. You won't be hearing about the planning permission they helped someone to sort out (dull), the reconciliation they brought to internecine strife in a certain part of town (just doing their job), or the endorsements they have given to help local businesses (presumed).

Often people ridicule politicians *en masse* as money and power-grabbers, but when you ask them about their own local MP they will say, 'Oh, she's wonderful. She does a lot of good work for the community. She has been so supportive of our projects. If only they were all like her.' We don't seem to be able to connect the micro and macro because of our faulty thinking. It illustrates precisely how much our attitudes can be influenced, assuming that most of what we read is true, and more importantly that what we read is the whole story. We seem unable to spot the reason that there is a difference between what we glean from our own first-hand experience of a local MP and what we glean through the filter of the media about all the others! More importantly we have developed the belief that what we are told as 'news' has somehow been downloaded from on high, rather than being the product of human, potentially sales-influenced decision-making. A further worrying development in this vicious feeding-frenzy is the prominence on TV news channels and websites of the top five clicked stories. A quick perusal of what one's fellow humans are most attracted to leaves you in no doubt that popularity does not equal significance or depth. Stories involving celebrities, sex or other visual stimulation inevitably lead the way. The self-fulfilling, people-pleasing cycle created leaves editors with even less room to manoeuvre when less sexy, but more worthy stories come along.

In my experience, exactly because they are accountable to their constituents, by way of elections and much direct communication, MPs and councillors do mostly know the reality of what is going on in their areas more than anyone. MPs are very aware of 'where the juice is flowing' in their constituencies and they know that it is often through the church and other Christian agencies.

Being an MP

There is another angle on the wider story, which is often missed, namely how demanding the role of an MP actually is. The majority have to work in two very separate geographical locations, with two very different groups of people. Constituencies can be many, many hours from London. This split means that they have to work hard to hold family life and relationships together. Then there is the added pressure of 24-hour media scrutiny of everything they say and do. Can you imagine if everything you ever said was reported or misreported, then surgically deconstructed?

We also grossly overestimate an MP's ability to effect local change, creating unrealistic and unfair expectations. For example, as a GP, when someone comes into your surgery, there is a basic unspoken understanding that the problem will be medical. This means that through their training and experience the GP will be able to accurately deduce the problem. They also have tools to hand, such as prescriptions for drugs and referrals to specialists. However, when a constituent walks into an MP's surgery, the situation is very different. Their issue may be about anything from bin collections, to schools, to green spaces, to third world debt. Not only is the breadth of understanding required huge, but the crucial fact is that an MP holds no official post of responsibility in their locality. They do not run any of the local councils. They are not the chief constable, or head of the chamber of commerce. They have a staff to answer correspondence but not to execute their wishes locally. Their tools are very limited. Any impact that they have on situations comes through the influence of letter-writing and relationship-building. But as we all know, relationships take time to build, meaning more meetings and gatherings in a week than many of us would manage in a few months.

The scale of the emotional engagement required is also huge. People often write to their MP as a last resort, so the problems they are describing are usually quite severe. Or the views they are expressing on a particular subject are rather passionate! MPs are humans too, and are not unaffected by what they read.

Are you starting to see why these people might need more of our support rather than just our complaints? Having observed many MPs at work, I want them better resourced and better staffed, rather than the opposite. I don't know about you, but I don't want overworked, sleep-deprived, stressed out, media-hounded people who are isolated from their families making my laws. I want people making my laws who have time to experience community life to the full and who have some space to reflect on things deeper than their Twitter feed. That way they are picking up on the realities of normal life, rather than being stuck in a Westminster bubble.

The GP analogy also holds for another common complaint about politicians. When I am campaigning I often hear this, 'The only time you hear from politicians is when they're looking for your vote. We never see them round here any other time. Then they're all over us.' At this point, I often try to politely point out that this constant attention would be impossible, if not even counter-productive. People don't expect their GP to simply wander around housing estates knocking on every door, asking if there is anyone sick in the house. Even the idea of it is ridiculous. So why do we expect it of our MPs? On average GPs have about 2,500 people on their lists, and yet people know that GPs have to prioritise those who are sick. They do this by having surgeries where those most in need can make their needs known. So how far-fetched is it to expect an MP whose constituency may cover a huge area, and probably about 70,000 people, to be personally checking up on everyone? That is why all MPs also run surgeries week-by-week, where those in need of help can make their case. Many do not, however, avail themselves of this opportunity, preferring instead to have something to moan about. This is our consumerised, sofa-based culture expressing itself again.

In or out?

I am not going to pretend that at times the word 'dirty' is not an accurate descriptor of party politics. Displays of tribalism, power-hungry ambition and economy with the truth cannot be ignored. But we have to ask ourselves whether we truly desire the political system to be cleaned up? Because that is much more likely to happen when those who have that passion for cleanliness become involved. As yet, my bath has never got cleaner because I have stood outside it, shaking my head wearily at the state it's in and speaking cleanness over it. (I keep praying!) It gets clean when I get into it and scrub it. Our engagement, or lack of it, reveals how much we really care. Will we simply critique like Pharisees, or serve like Jesus? The salt and light thing really works. Light does illuminate darkness. Salt does preserve the meat. In fact, if you do believe that politics is a dark, dirty world, surely there could no better place for God's light to be shining?

Throughout Scripture we read how God has used his people – people like Joseph, Daniel and Obadiah – to bring wisdom, truth and justice to appalling regimes. The dirt did not deter them. When folks question whether they could be involved in our current system of politics, I point them towards Nebuchadnezzar's horrendous regime and suggest that Daniel had plenty of excuses to not get involved. Another point to note is that more often than not the prophets of the Old Testament operated not at a distance, but in proximity to the leaders of the nations. They were in good relationship with kings and princes. They were close enough to be asked for wisdom at key moments, or close enough to volunteer prophetic critique before it was too late.

Yes, there are particular challenges to morality in the world of politics, but there are similar challenges in every subculture. In business, people are tempted to put profit before people, self-employed people are tempted to fiddle their taxes, in music, people can sacrifice their sexuality to grab attention, and so on. Having had the privilege of operating in a few different spheres, I honestly believe the world of politics is no more or less corrupt than any other sphere of human existence. But some of the particular challenges I see in politics are these:

- Lust for power leading to unbridled selfish ambition.
- The need to beat someone else to achieve your ends, leading to spin and point-scoring.
- Compromise of principle for expediency, or popularity.
- The co-option of a rights-based individualism.

None of these challenges are insurmountable, and I see a new generation of believers who are getting involved and already moving in the opposite spirit. Together, it is possible. These strongholds that develop are reasons to be prayerfully involved, not reasons to run in the opposite direction.

No-go areas?

For Christians to live as though certain areas of life are no-go areas is dangerous. It risks the moral fracture of those areas. In fact, many commentators would argue that the state of our nation presently is a direct result of the church of the 1960s and 1970s stepping back from political life. How can we complain about what we have now if back then we simply sat tutting on the sidelines? Mentally limiting the areas over which God and his people can have influence has led to a safe retreat from public engagement in so many areas. Abraham Kuyper famously challenged this faulty thinking: 'There is not a square inch of domain of our human existence over which Christ, who is sovereign over all, does not cry: "It is Mine!" '[1]

Every sphere of life is simultaneously glorious and fallen, and we waste our time by avoiding certain spheres as a whole rather than desiring their restoration. We also need a dose of humility

---

[1] Abraham Kuyper, *A Centennial Reader*.

at this point. If politics is guilty of the abuse of power, the church is not immune as the history books (even recent history books) sadly show. Surely this makes it clear that our seasonal picking on different spheres or groups can be unhelpful. We are always keener to blame someone else for our problems. We must critique immoral practice, but the wholesale rubbishing first of politicians, then newspapers, then unions, then bankers and so on and so on, leaves us feeling powerless and misses the fundamental point. As Alexander Solzhenitsyn said, 'But the line dividing good and evil cuts through the heart of every human being'.[2] The common and most significant factor in flawed systems and professions is the presence of human sinfulness. And as a race we aren't confined to just one area of life. Any systems involving human beings will have similar dysfunctions. There is always selfish ambition, lack of ability to see the other side of an argument, and self-protection that stymies the common good. These inevitably lead to power struggles, back-biting, herd mentalities, and corruption. Sadly anyone who is a member of a church knows this all too well.

Recently I was speaking to a Christian conference audience with my 'partner in crime' Colin Bloom (Director of the Conservative Christian Fellowship). During the Q and A session a gentleman stood up to make a statement that was tremendously revealing. He explained that the reason Christians shouldn't and didn't get involved in politics was that they could see that power corrupted people, and therefore it was better to do jobs of leadership within the church and Christian organisations. It was fascinating to see the false sacred/secular divide in play. It is incredibly naïve of us to believe that the same power dynamics that people in 'the real world' are subject to, do not happen in the church! In fact any member of any church can probably tell you plenty of sore stories about how they have seen power abused. Do we seriously think we are staying pure from those dynamics by staying in a Christian bubble? There is wonderful servant leadership in many churches, but surely we

---

[2] Alexander Solzhenitsyn, *The Gulag Archipelago*, 1918–1956: An experiment in literary investigation (HarperCollins, London 1974).

should be bringing that to the world, to infuse the leadership of business and politics with those values, rather than hiding it away.

Another thing that frustrates me is the unspoken class war that goes on within politics. The underlying assumption of many attacks on 'the other side' is that they are somehow devious and less moral than we are. It is a much easier way to win than actually having to make an argument. Playing the man (or woman), not the ball, is all too common. So when some on the left lazily brand all bankers as corrupt, or some on the right lazily brand all unemployed people as scroungers, we are falling into the same trap. Do we really believe that one socio-economic group is more moral than another? Different people in different circumstances simply face different temptations. One is not more immoral than the other. Of course the influence that certain people have means that their mistakes have a wider impact than others, so legislatively you may need to focus more attention there, but this is not the point in contention here. The point is that to assume there are different degrees of fallenness in different parts of society is foolish. We need to be speaking prophetically of where the gospel grinds up against every subculture and sphere, rather than making scapegoats of the few.

Pantomime

It is unfortunate that our opinions about politics are so informed by the nonsense that is Prime Ministers' Questions – or what I call 'the Wednesday Pantomime'. It is more widely reported than anything else because of the potent cocktail of drama, warfare and celebrity that it provides. But it issues a very skewed picture of what MPs spend their time doing. If that was all they did, then you would understand peoples' antipathy to politics. Why would someone get involved in a trade where it seems that you would need to leave your faith at the door, never mind your intelligence or courtesy! But in time terms PMQs represents only about 1/100th of what MPs spend their week doing. It does not give an accurate reflection. All the moments of sober discussion, co-operation in committees, private meetings, socialising together, or praying together don't make good TV or column inches. A hungry public want controversy and fighting. The middle-classes crave their version of TV wrestling. However, none of this wider context excuses what PMQs has become or relinquishes the parties from the responsibility to revolutionise this interaction. The present speaker of the House of Commons has been keen to 'civilise' it, and as Christians in Politics we are hugely supportive of this. Having said all that, we should not forget that our adversarial parliamentary system does in general mean that successive governments are held to strict account. To be complaining about the pantomime is still much better than to be complaining about a brutal dictatorship.

6

BUT I CAN'T AGREE WITH EVERYTHING THAT PARTY STANDS FOR

He who surrenders himself without reservation to the temporal claims of a nation, or a party, or a class is rendering to Caesar that which, of all things, most emphatically belongs to God: himself.

C. S. Lewis, *Weight of Glory*

You're right. You can't. And neither can I. In fact I disagree quite profoundly with some things. But I put it to you that you probably don't agree with everything that your spouse, or your closest friends, believe, and you certainly don't agree with everything that everyone in your church believes, yet you work together, finding common cause for the greater good.

We are communal beings, designed in the image of our triune God to interact and work with others. As Father, Son and Holy Spirit, God represents unity in diversity. And yet so often we shy away from working with others who are not quite the same as us, as it is too much hard work. Co-operation with those who are exactly like us is much easier, to be honest. The bottom line is you are never going to agree with every policy on a party's policy slate. I know too many Christians who have spent too long procrastinating over which party to join – and I was one of them – based on a slightly messianic presumption that through their choice they will definitively decide the debate that has raged amongst Christians for hundreds of years. That is, which party is the right one for Christians to vote for. Or which political ideology is closest to what God wants. Human ideologies inevitably reflect both the glory of God and the fallenness of humanity to varying measure. They will never be perfect. If we wait around for the perfect party, we will be waiting a long time.

Having said all that, there is one party where I agree with 100% of their policies. But it's called the 'Andy Flannagan party'. It has only one member, sadly, and that's me. That is the philosophical thick end of the wedge of this type of separatist thinking. We believers often paint ourselves further and further into a corner until there is nowhere left to go. And no one left to go with.

Ever so subtly, I fear, we have been lulled into believing something that is altogether sinister. The drastically different concepts of acceptance and agreement have been subtly fused. Let me try to explain. Read any newspaper or web article and you will notice something interesting. Whenever two groups or two individuals disagree about something, there is an assumption that those individuals or groups are not in good relationship. We can't seem to believe that those who disagree on a certain issue will not be able to extend an arm of fellowship or embrace toward each other. Obviously this suits those who want to create fights and acrimony in headlines, but acceptance and agreement are simply not the same thing. It is dishonest to pretend that we agree with every opinion or life choice of those whom we accept and love. After all this acceptance is surely the basis of any healthy long-term relationship. Those relationships that start with honest disagreement often outlast those that are founded on eagerness to please.

The examples of this lazy thinking are legion. You could mention the exaggeration of Cabinet splits. Or you could talk about the party political drama that masks people working and socialising together across party lines.

Acceptance and agreement are not the same thing. It is possible to work alongside people with whom we disagree on certain subjects. We are not necessarily saying that we agree with them on everything. I wish we could all be more honest about this.

Of course we need to be careful of the trappings of power, and the compromises we may be tempted to make, but that does not mean we should avoid getting involved at all. Instead, this is a reason to make sure Christians go into politics as communities, as communities with a mission, rather than as individuals. There are Christians on the Left groups, Conservative Christian Fellowship groups and Liberal Democrat Christian Forum groups all over the country which provide support, prayer, theological resources and practical help for those who are engaged. We need to keep our saltiness, or, as we know, we become useless.

To effect change, we need to co-operate with those with whom we may not necessarily agree on everything. In fact, that is where the excitement is. That is where prayer and faith are required. Our ideas and presuppositions get challenged, sending us back to Scripture and causing us to flesh out the Word. Shock horror – we may also actually learn something from others. And this co-operation provides an incredible mission field. We genuinely share life with fellow travellers rather than keeping to our own set.

In our brash and immediate Twitterised world, the art of persuasion needs to be rediscovered. Building real relationships is key. If someone is persuaded of something, they then start living in line with their new thinking. This is not the case if they merely capitulate to our strength of numbers or volume. The art of shouting from a distance may also have its place at times, but something tells me we don't need as much practice at that one.

Party on

The acute observer of party politics spots fairly quickly the issue that for many Christians seems to be a deal breaker. The issue is party loyalty. The argument goes something like this. There will be times when your faith will go against the party line. Therefore you are on a hiding to nothing. The whipping system forces everyone to stay in line. You will become a robot rather than a thinking individual. You will compromise.

The whipping system is portrayed as a vice-like mechanism designed to squeeze the individuality out of MPs. I cannot vouch for some of the methods applied by whips to get their members into line. Clearly there have been bullying tactics used at times, but this is the exception rather than the rule. There is, in fairness, much to critique, but again I think we need to see it in context and hear the other side of the story.

To listen to the criticism of some, you would think that their ideal scenario would be MPs being able to vote however they wanted on any given piece of legislation. But imagine what it would be like if there were 650 independent MPs in parliament. You would hardly ever get any legislation passed. Also any legislation passed would rarely sit in a coherent narrative, meaning that laws could be counter-productive or damaging to previously made legislation. Leadership would be very difficult in this context (it is difficult enough with a party system!). Running a government effectively without a sense of loyalty would be almost impossible. Just ask anyone who runs a business or a school how hard it is to steer the ship without some degree of 'encouraged' loyalty!

To get anything done for the good of everyone in a country or a town, you have to find common cause with others. You have to build coalitions. Each of the mainstream parties are a coalition of many smaller clans. There are times when they speak with great harmony, but there are times when there is great discord. Arguments happen – sometimes in private, often in public – to thrash out what the 'party line' will be on a given subject. It is then a principle of collective responsibility that leads people to back the party line even if their own opinion differs from it. We see this in the Cabinets of town councils and the Cabinet of the country. There will be disagreements, but when the decision is made, stability is often better served by members collectively owning the decision. Some debates will go your way and some will not. When the decisions do go your way, you are glad of the collective responsibility factor to stop your plans being thwarted. The reality is that it is no different in church leadership teams. They will have robust discussions about many subjects, but once they have decided a shared direction, it is the job of the team to communicate and facilitate that, even if they have some misgivings.

Of course there may be times when we simply cannot agree, and we believe the issue is of such importance that we cannot stay in the vicinity of those who are advocating it. In such cases there may be a price to be paid, but this is part of the reality of political life.

One of the people who was instrumental in allowing me an insight into the world of politics was Andy Reed, the former MP for Loughborough. The first MP's surgery I ever sat in on was with him in his constituency. He experienced the pain and the peace of differing from the party line on an important subject. In 2003, he was a Parliamentary Private Secretary (PPS) to Gordon Brown and thereby a member of the government. It's a job that involves helping a prominent member of the cabinet with a wide number of tasks, and is usually a first rung on the ministerial jobs ladder. Andy however could not square his conscience with the decision to support the USA in the Iraq war. He felt so strongly about it, that he had no other option but to resign. Many others confided to him that they agreed but they did not have the nerve to resign. No matter what you think about the Iraq war, what was it about Andy Reed that gave him the nerve to do so? Surely it was partly an understanding that he was accountable to a higher power and that even though his career would suffer, this was not the most important factor in the final analysis.

At this point it is worth pointing out that we need to be careful about the use of the word 'moral'. Many in the church describe their lines in the sand as 'the moral issues'; meaning abortion, marriage or euthanasia. While I share a belief in the importance of these issues, there is a real danger in saying that these are *the* moral issues. I believe war is a moral issue. I believe how we organise our economy is a profoundly moral issue. This false dichotomy has been part of why the church has failed to make an impact on certain issues.

So although there are times to take a stand, in a world where conflict and misunderstanding are so prevalent, we should be the ones who are enthusiastic about finding common cause with others. As we noted earlier, a great example of the church being at the heart of finding common cause with others of goodwill has been the phenomenon of community organising. We believe human beings are made in the image of God, and therefore will reflect his creativity and wisdom to some extent. But, for too long, as the church, we have believed that we have a monopoly on good ideas. Thankfully we do often have good ideas, but sadly we often don't have enough experience in governance to turn those ideas into practical policy and later law. Here lies the relational and skills gap we are addressing throughout this book. Salt can only do its job as a preservative when it is rubbed into the meat. A separate pile of salt does no work at all. A torch has no impact in a brightly lit room. A church working only with Christians is no church at all.

Also, we can learn and benefit from the wisdom of others. We are told in Proverbs,

> 'As iron sharpens iron,
> so one person sharpens another.'
> Proverbs 27:17

We can be refined and honed by those around us, whoever they are, whether they have faith or not, if only we would meaningfully interact with them.

This refining is hugely important because politics is a complicated business. Just as a missionary to a new culture has to learn the new language, so believers must learn the language of politics and governance. You cannot simply walk into rooms and expect people to understand every word you say. Claiming that a statement is true because the Bible says so may convince fellow believers, but may sound nonsensical to those who don't believe. Your values and principles will need some translation to be heard and more importantly understood. You will need to learn the language and the criteria of politics. A Christian plumber can't ignore learning about pipes and valves just because he is a Christian. Just saying 'be healed' to a blocked sink may work, but my experience is that mostly it doesn't. Similarly a Christian entering politics must learn the pipes and valves of legislation and governance.

This is an area where we have some thinking to do as Christians. Law-making is not simply decided by what is right and wrong. You cannot take Scripture straight off the shelf and throw it into legislation. For example, as Christians we believe that adultery is wrong. In fact so do most people. But should it be against the law? What would be the impact of the law? How would you police it? Would it divert scarce resources away from other areas of policing or the courts? Is it the best way to encourage fidelity? For many issues like this there is a job of translation to be done to work out what best serves the common good practically, yet still holds true to the principles we do dearly believe in. Those are often not easy answers, and Christians will often come to very different conclusions about many of them. And that is okay.

That is why the Christian groupings within the parties are putting such an emphasis on training. We want to see character and competence built into our 'missionaries'. Operating in this way also avoids the mistakes made by missionaries of the past who never stopped to understand the cultures they set foot in. They assumed that all of culture was 'fallen' rather than looking for the good in it. If instead we go in listening there is a real chance that more people will come to know Jesus in the midst of our mission, for that is how he operated, working with people, rather than doing things to them without their agency. It is much more likely that we will be playing our part in God's mission rather than dragging him into ours.

Change from the inside

A further more obvious point in this area is that if there are policies that we disagree with in a certain party, then how will those policies be changed unless people like us get involved in making the arguments within the party? At times your voice is heard much more clearly when you whisper from a place of relationship, than rant from a distance.

Let's focus on the detail of our present political spectrum for a moment. Let me explain why I believe Christians are needed more than ever within our political parties. The impact of newspapers siding with left or right, and increasingly news channels doing the same, cannot be overestimated. There is a polarising effect on our public discourse. On many programmes, whether it is for the discussion of an issue, or simply reviewing the papers, the panel consists of someone from the right and someone from the left. It is in the interests of TV and radio producers and journalists to engender as much hostility as possible, as it makes for a great programme. There are many times when I have been asked to appear on radio or TV, but after an initial conversation with a researcher they have decided I am too 'nuanced' for their programme. It's not that I don't have strong views, it's just that they don't always fit in their prescribed boxes. They don't want someone on air who may attempt to reconcile, or see the good in the other argument. They don't necessarily want someone who is going to be friendly even while disagreeing. They often want someone who is going to stir things up. They want someone who will get listeners or viewers calling in because they have made them irate with a certain opinion or the way it was expressed. They want the firestorm it will create on Twitter.

The hostility encouraged by mainstream media and then reinforced by social media scares people further into their tribes – broadly progressive (tending towards change) or conservative (tending towards keeping things the same). It's much safer to adhere to the assumptions of your tribe because you will have their support when you stick your head above the parapet. And you need lots of it because in the world of social media, once your head is above the parapet, it will definitely get shot at.

The lack of genuine relationship-building at the heart of much social media interaction leads this warfare to be all the more antagonistic. For example, observe the incredible flak taken by Mehdi Hassan when he shared his views on abortion in the *New Statesman*.[1] Or on the other side, the abuse hurled at Philip Blond (who was dubbed 'global village idiot of the net') when he dared to question some sacred cows of capitalism. The tribes are very fast to 'eat their own' to preserve their own philosophical purity.

The greatest number of consecutive minutes I have ever spent on Twitter was during the Olympic opening ceremony in 2012. That evening I got a scary insight into how Twitter sometimes operates. It can be basically like a school playground. People meander around saying not very much at all, occasionally hovering in the general vicinity of the cool people to pick up whatever they may say. Then someone says something that is politically incorrect or uncool, and people round on them. People who have no connection to the transgressor come flying over from the other side of the playground to drive the knife in. No one really knows the context of what was actually said or done.

There is a real danger in the UK that we slide further towards the American phenomenon of a self-cannibalising media. Cable news networks are full of discussions based on controversies that have arisen from what someone else said on another news network. The news becomes about words rather than actions.

So how do we avoid joining in this tribal warfare? Our primary tribal identity must be in Jesus. We are in his tribe. It has to be Kingdom first and earthly tribes second. One way of making sure this happens is by regularly reading Scripture. As I listen or read I am regularly surprised by the words I hear. God is so much more surprising than I give him credit for. He cannot be owned or boxed by one tribe or another. If you read Scripture and keep reading it, it would appear God is more passionate about our personal devotion and miracles than some of my more liberal friends would like, and more radical about economic justice and creation care than some of my more conservative friends would

---

[1] http://www.newstatesman.com/lifestyle/lifestyle/2012/10/being-pro-life-doesnt-make-me-any-less-lefty (accessed 11 October 2012).

like. As far as I can see, God cares equally about what goes on in boardrooms and bedrooms.

Tom Wright points out that we will always need progressive moments and conservative moments.[2] History is littered with examples when both have been significant. To pretend that one is always more important than the other is intellectually vacuous. The danger lies in getting lost in one tribe or the other, abandoning our need to consult God on any given issue, and instead just adopting the instinctive tribal reaction. The Twitter- and blogosphere is sadly littered with instant knee-jerk reactions rather than responses based on mature reflection or prayer.

One thing to note however (and I say this as someone who works with the Labour party) is that it is much rarer for conservative moments to be heralded in the history books. Please note that when I use the word conservative in this section, I don't mean the party, I mean the ethos, although there is of course some crossover. Stopping a certain behaviour because you want to prevent something bad from happening is much less sexy and exciting, and, because the bad thing you prevented from happening didn't happen, no one appreciates the fact that you stopped it. The smoke alarm designer gets far less public acknowledgement than the firefighter. The people who set speed limits don't get the same credit as the paramedics who pick up the pieces. The people of faith whose traditions have held societies together for centuries, bringing at least some small sense of community and equality, get far less credit than the activists behind the next emancipation campaign.

We are all products of our history and cultures and we do need to be questioning and assessing which traditions and roots we should be cherishing and which roots we should be tearing out for the compost heap. The lazy, blind progressive has no roots left. The lazy, blind conservative has a field full of weeds.

So can you see why Christians can have such a powerful influence in all of the political parties? They can be part of ensuring

---

[2] Tom Wright, *How God Became King* (SPCK, London 2012).

that they do not slide wholesale into this oversimplified tribal warfare with its attendant philosophical vacuum.

Of course having said all of the above, we shouldn't lose track of the fact that to be part of a party in any meaningful way, our membership should not be arbitrary. We will only be motivated participants with some degree of integrity if a substantial portion of what the party stands for connects with our own values. Otherwise our engagement will be half-hearted and we may stand accused of our engagement being a clandestine Trojan Horse strategy!

Christians coming to the party

At this point you might be thinking, 'But you could solve this problem if you had a Christian party.' Then it could avoid the tribal problems. Would it? In my experience, and according to many surveys, it would appear Christians have as wide a spread of opinions on most issues as normal citizens. As we mentioned in a previous chapter, the breakdown of voting statistics shows that Christians' voting patterns are just as tied to their family and cultural background they are to as their theological positions. It is possible to disagree over the interpretation of many pieces of Scripture, and even if you agree on the interpretation, it is still entirely possible to disagree on how and whether it should be translated into law.

I admire much of the work done by certain Christian parties in the last couple of decades. At times it has been impressively rigorous and deeply thought through. I want to commend any Christians getting off the sofa and getting involved.

However my argument here would be the salt and light one. All that political energy and genius is wasted to the mainstream parties if it is locked up within Christian parties. All those evangelistic opportunities are lost because we are generally not rubbing shoulders with folks who don't believe. There is also a pragmatic point about the UK political system, which, after the failed Alternative Vote referendum, now looks very unlikely to change for some time. (Of course this is a personal view, but at the time of the vote, the Church of England steered clear of the debate, not least as it appeared an energy and cash-sapping distraction from the issues facing the country, and the wider and deeper questions of lack of public engagement and trust in the political world.) Our first past the post system makes it very difficult for small parties to achieve a level of influence in keeping with their support. The best (or worst) example of this was in 1983 when the SDP-Liberal Alliance scored 25% of the popular vote but only 4% of the seats in Parliament. It would be almost impossible for a 'Christian' party to make any headway. The same sadly applies to independent candidates and smaller parties. I share many of the aspirations of those who wish to see mainstream politics shaken out of its sense of entitlement. I enjoy seeing the Establishment challenged as we are seeing at present. But with our present system if we are serious as the church about having meaningful influence, we need to have a solid Christian presence in the main parties. Whether we like it or not, they will form our governments for very many years.

When we think about Christian parties we also need to wonder about that tag 'Christian' being applied to any inanimate object. I believe people can be Christians, but can you have a Christian street, or town or country? That is a topical moot point, but surely we can agree that the creation of lots of separate 'Christian' versions of mainstream structures has not necessarily served us well; 'Christian' newspapers, 'Christian' art, 'Christian' aerobics? What if instead of forming separate cultures or industries we allowed more of the God-given creativity of believers to infuse the mainstream?

I think there is also a potential philosophical problem with Christian parties. The logical successful endgame of a Christian party would in effect be a theocracy. And theocracies don't have a great history, or present. As God's people, are we called to lord it over the unbelievers or are we called to serve amongst them, providing wisdom and leadership?

More widely, for the church to be closely aligned to a Christian political party is unhelpful in at least two ways: Firstly, it may suggest that Christians make better rulers, which is far from proven. The goal is not just to get Christians into power but to have righteous and effective government. Secondly, if a church, or a group of churches, is identified with a single party, that makes it more difficult for church members and other Christians to oppose that party. Herron is right when he says 'God is not on the side of any political party but on the side of justice, compassion, truth, mercy, freedom and life'.

Speak up for whom?

This is a good place to mention what I believe can be one of the glorious distinctives of Christians in the public square. We are in an age where every minority group is loudly fighting for their rights, and the more loudly and outrageously they fight for them, often the more effective they are. Radio station phone-ins are full of people demanding their rights, and discussions become a trade-off between differing 'rights'. As Christians we cannot allow ourselves to become just another minority fighting for our rights. Our arguments will become increasingly shrill, and we will end up playing power games rather than learning the art of persuasion. Of course we must articulate what we believe is best for our nation, but framing it in terms of 'our rights' falls into a philosophical and strategic trap. We need to reject much of a rights-based culture as followers of the one who gave up his rights for the greater good, while acknowledging that the concept of 'human rights' (based on Biblical precedent) has enabled huge strides forward for the human race.

Our beautiful distinctive inspired by the well-known proverb (Proverbs 31:8) is that we are called not to just to speak up for ourselves, but to speak up for those who cannot speak for themselves. It really confuses people when we do this. Folks cannot understand why we would spend our precious time arguing on behalf of someone else. I have seen this strategy be hugely effective many times when I have been the 'token Christian' on Radio 5 late night phone-in debates. Be it discussions about bullying, pornography, royalty or war, it is amazing how it is difficult to argue against you when you are actually speaking up on behalf of others. For example when talking about pornography, the interviewer is hoping for me to take a moralising line to assault the porn magazine editor who is up 'against' me. He is flummoxed when instead I talk about the struggles of some of the young people who we work with in the church, who are bombarded with sexualised imagery. Speaking on their behalf spoke volumes, and left my 'opponent' with nowhere to go. We have much to learn in navigating the new media public square, and I cannot claim to be an expert, but I do know that doing it in a way that only represents Christians is not the answer. We descend into lowest common denominator territory when we start to use phrases like, 'They wouldn't do that to the Muslims. We need a show of force.' In the kingdom, ends don't justify means. Our attempts at persuasion cannot be about fear.

At the last election, some agencies used an interesting model to attempt to influence politicians. Politicians were scored on their voting on certain 'Christian' issues. At this point, I would refer you back to our discussion about 'moral' issues. To call certain issues 'Christian' is to preclude the possibility of God having an opinion about things like foreign policy or immigration. More significantly, MPs were given a point score and asked to sign a declaration. None of the Christian groups in parliament were consulted about the declaration, it should be noted. Christians were encouraged to sign it themselves and email their MPs to let them know. This is what I call 'muscle-based' campaigning. And it works pretty well in the USA. It works pretty well there because there is less of a broad church of political views amongst Christians, but also because in the USA, they have the numbers to make it work. For the UK, I think it is not always the best way to go about things not only in relational terms, but also strategically, because, quite simply, we don't have the numbers.

If we are to persuade a majority of people to be in favour of a certain position, we will have to *persuade* them. We can't just invest in the logistics and mechanics of getting our vote out. Persuasion is achieved through relationship, and through occupying strategic positions. Again, don't hear me wrong. We need the challenging prophetic voices. Conventional wisdom can become all too pervasive. One can't help but notice the higher than usual number of amendments that have been needed by the Lords in recent years because of legislative lapses. But we need those voices to be working in tandem with those on the inside. Sadly those relationships are not what they could or should be yet. Please pray for that to change and for all of us involved to confess our failures and faults. It is also all too easy for those 'on the inside' to become so acclimatised to conventional wisdom that their challenging voice becomes neutered. At that point, it doesn't matter how good your relationships are!

The system

You may still be thinking that you could not associate with a certain party because of certain policies, be that a policy on marriage, the market or healthcare. The desire to distance ourselves from these policies is understandable as it usually based on another fear – namely that we will be compromised by being associated. But I have news for those who say that through our involvement in the political system we will inevitably be corrupted by the system. We *are* all inevitably corrupted by the system.

To pretend that as Christians we can somehow sit outside the systems of our world to keep ourselves pure is quite simply nonsense. Every time you fill a car with petrol, you are supporting some very questionable Middle Eastern states, many of which are oppressing women and persecuting believers. Every time you shop at a huge supermarket, you may be endorsing the destruction of high streets and enabling the shoddy treatment of food suppliers, both local and global. Every time you invest, you might end up supporting a company like Wonga. We live in a fallen world where perfect choices for purest outcomes simply cannot be made. To be virtuous in such a scenario is either to take material self-denial to unsustainable levels or to commit to living in constant state of critical self-awareness around the choices we make. Life is complex; global financial arrangements more so. The Modern

Slavery Bill shows we need to – and can – be alert to and committed to legislating against some of the worst effects at the other end of those chains that we join as consumers.

Every time you pay for a newspaper, re-order your broadband, organise your pension, visit your GP, or renew your house insurance, you are more deeply embedded in the disturbing, complex, yet redeemable (and they will inevitably be redeemed) structures of our world. You can't avoid it. You are part of the system and you are supporting it by your mere existence.

The question is not whether or not we should get involved. We are involved! The question is whether you sit passively just letting it all happen, removing yourself into a supposed pure space that isn't really pure at all, or whether you act to change things. For some reason we draw these intellectually incoherent lines to that say we can associate ourselves intimately through a mortgage with a bank who are benefitting from arms trading, but not with a party whose policy we disagree with on a certain subject. Abstaining from involvement is totally legitimate in either case, but we should be consistent.

It is perhaps possible to remove yourself to some extent from the fallen systems and structures of this world. In fact over the centuries many have tried through monasteries or retreat centres. They often grow all their own food so as not to increase human consumption of an already fragile planet, but they will still need expert input at times from outside. It is very hard to completely detach. Much of this sort of life actually attracts me because of its simplicity. It has a lot to teach us of contemplation in the midst of our frenetic modern lives, but surely the challenge is to integrate those disciplines into our interaction with the world as it is. Our hope and prayer must be that in those dangerous interactions (for we may indeed be polluted) that light will prove itself more powerful than darkness. I believe it surely is, but I am also aware that I am often the one who dims the light in my fallenness. As we engage with society do we really believe it when we read 'he who is in you is greater than he who is in the world' (1 John 4:4 ESV)? If we did, we would engage the principalities and powers with some confidence, rather than fearfully hiding in our own little worlds.

Responsibility

As we mentioned earlier, we have at times allowed ourselves to become the postcard-senders who are never sent. Our minds have adjusted to a position of permanent protest, instead of a place of responsibility. Possibly because it's easier.

The difference that responsibility makes is huge. We are easily lulled into a culture that is screaming for its rights. It is not surprising, as we have been suckered into seeing our role in life as consumers. I will give an example from my own experience. I was on my medical elective in 1995 in Cairo. We were working in a hospital in the 'rubbish city' of Mokattam. It was 42 degrees when we arrived and I was struck down by a nasty tummy bug. Every night when we got home my solace was tuning into the BBC World Service news at 11pm. One UK story making the world service news that summer was from my hometown. There was a stand-off at Drumcree church between the Orangemen who wanted to walk down a traditional parade route through a Catholic area, and the police who were caught in between keeping the peace. The conflict escalated to the point that Northern Ireland ground to a standstill, with Loyalists erecting roadblocks all over the country. That year the Orangemen won and an abiding visual memory for many was David Trimble and Ian Paisley (unionist leaders) striding through the High Street of Portadown to rapturous cheers, arms raised together.

Fast forward a couple of years. As the result of the Good Friday Agreement, David Trimble is now First Minister of Northern Ireland. His deputy is the nationalist SDLP deputy leader Seamus Mallon. The Drumcree stand-off is happening again. This time I'm watching it on TV live. People are getting injured and normal life is again grinding to a halt around Northern Ireland. But this time David Trimble is sitting at a press conference with Seamus Mallon and they are together advocating calm, recommending that everything possible be done to forge a peaceful compromise. No more the previous talk of inalienable unionist rights being violated, which had encouraged the protests to continue. Things have settled down.

Do you see the impact that responsibility brings? In his previous role as unionist party leader and without formal governing responsibility, David Trimble was more of a shop steward or cheerleader for a cause. In those sorts of roles, to ensure you remain as the leader, you need to gain some attention by being as hard line as possible. However, when the nation's wellbeing was, to an extent, in his hands, he stepped back to see the big picture and stepped up. In working with others we are forced to see their side of the picture. But the key is that we often need to be working with them, sharing some responsibility. If we stay in our silos, we miss out on the learning, and we also reduce the opportunity for others to rub shoulders with us, and also the opportunity for them to pick up that smell of Jesus that we are supposed to carry. You will be surprised by how much common ground there is, and you will also be surprised by how much God's people shine. I feel we need a collective intravenous bolus of confidence in the church in the UK. Some of the projects that we are involved in are simply breathtaking, and the caring, creative, efficient, professional, organic leaders that are being produced put the monotone products of the modern political machine in the shade. We have an incredible head start. Let's use it. Let's be sent into the mission field of politics.

7

SHOWING UP:
LIZZIE JEWKES

L et me introduce you to Lizzie Jewkes. She is a 57-year-old
mother of four living in Whitby, just outside Chester. Meeting
her has been one of the highlights of my year, because she is
an incredible example of putting what we have been talking about
into practice.

For Lizzie, her political journey is inseparable from her faith
journey, so she enthusiastically told me how it all started. She
remembers, as a five-year-old at a Sunday School service, hearing
'some bloke' talking about 'having Jesus in your life'. She walked
home excitedly to tell her mum this good news, but was gazumped
by her brother (two years her senior) who announced before
her that he wanted Jesus in his life. Three years later,
another significant memory was the coverage of the 1966
General Election and Lizzie was unimpressed by Harold Wilson
'cosying up' to the unions, as she saw it. At that point she was only
eight years old! For the rest of her childhood, she attended a free
church with her mum, but on leaving home became an Anglican.
She now worships at a charismatic Anglican church plant based in
a local school.

In 1984, aged 27, Lizzie was incensed by someone from the
Labour party campaigning at her little girl's nursery. She was given
balloons to hold for what she described as a 'propaganda photo'
but was told that the nursery would close if she didn't join up to

a campaign against rate capping. She felt manipulated and this triggered her into political activism. As she enquired about council cuts, she quickly noticed that a lot of men were making decisions that advantaged men. Cuts were being made to services that were mostly used or staffed by women – home helps, childminders, meals on wheels, libraries, and swimming pools.

She was also inspired by political figures who stood up for what they believed, no matter the consequences, such as Dick Taverne, who resigned from the Labour party to stand as an independent. She remembers sitting up all night to watch his count. As a teenager, she had decided that the Liberal party was closest to her principles and joined them. She wanted votes at 16, more care for the environment (when no one was talking about it), proportional representation and a fairer system of rates. She is very loyal to her party in general but described assisted dying as an issue she could not go along with (along with many in other parties) if it was proposed.

Since then she has spent a lot of her time attending local Liberal and LibDem branch meetings. She stands at every local election but has never managed to get elected onto the local council – no LibDems ever have in her area. In four separate Westminster elections she has also stood as the LibDem candidate.

Through all her campaigning, Lizzie has become known locally as someone who gets things done. People come to her with problems because they know she will take them seriously, and has the relationships necessary to effect change. Among the many issues she has 'sorted' for locals are signs for local amenities, problems with bollards and people camping illegally on the land.

When I asked her why it is was better for her to be doing this with a political hat on rather than as part of a church group she said, 'People recognise you are part of a broader enterprise. There is some accountability that comes with that. Last week I was being told about problems with some local traffic lights. If I was just a church group I would not be as approachable. It also enables me to help everybody. There are always people who want nothing to do with the church.' But she is not apologetic about her faith.

When people ask her why she does what she does, she is happy to tell them that it is because she is a Christian and thereby has a responsibility to make people's lives as good as possible and to stand up to vested interests and corruption.

When she reflects on her story she can see that politics was in her blood. She describes her mum as a 'raving Tory', as was her grandad (if slightly less raving). Her auntie was a Liberal local councillor. There were no sermons or books that convinced her that politics was a valid vocation for a Christian. She simply thought that it was obvious that Christians should be standing up to what was so obviously wrong. For her, a big part of this was the closed shop. She knew folks who had attended job interviews and had been turned down because they were not members of the union. She also detested the monopolies of uncaring big businesses. She was into Fairtrade in the 1980s, 'long before it was cool'. To her it just seemed obvious that you should pay people a fair wage.

The Bible story that provides Lizzie with most inspiration is that of Elijah and the prophets of Baal. She admired the fact that Elijah stood against everyone and against huge logistical odds simply because he knew what was right.

Lizzie's life already seems inspiring enough to me, but pin back your ears.

When this part of her story begins she was working for a temping agency having recently lost her job. Previously she had worked for various charities, run her own café and set up a washable nappy business.

She was at the Liberal Democrat party conference in 2008 not long after Nick Clegg had been elected leader. He announced that he reckoned he could save £20BN across various Government departments and give it back in tax. His radical idea was to reduce income tax rate from 20p to 16p in the pound. Many had concerns, but the policy was voted through because he was a new leader. But the gentleman sitting next to her said, 'Why did we do that? If we have £20BN to help people we should raise the income tax threshold. (The earning limit below which you do not have to pay income tax.) That would help people most in need.' Lizzie thought this was a brilliant idea, but he then added that it would be impossible to do.

As she thought and prayed about it, she became more and more convinced of the idea. At the time the threshold was just over £6,000. Her perception was that the tax shake-up when the lower 10p tax rate was removed had, in general, helped men and not women. With all the Bible verses about the poor and vulnerable ringing in her ears she said she could not imagine how someone making £120 a week could afford to give the government something back. She wanted the level of the threshold to be raised to £11,137, equivalent to the minimum wage. In other words if you are being paid exactly the minimum wage full-time you would have no income tax to pay. She calculated that people would be £800 a year better off. Her further rationale for the policy was that lower paid people would spend any money they are given, benefitting their local economies, whereby richer folks would tend to save it.

Here the advantages of Lizzie's party membership become clear. She knew that the senior Liberal Democrat MP Vince Cable was speaking at an event near where she lived, so she planned to 'nobble' him. She grabbed him at the end of the meeting and presented her idea to him. He confided, 'That's my ultimate dream, but I don't think we could afford it.'

She was encouraged, but unsure where to go next.

A few weeks later she received an email from Jo Swinson MP on behalf of the LibDem womens' network. It was requesting input on policy ideas. She forwarded her increasingly thought-through plan and they really liked it.

Jo was then able to give Lizzie access to helpful information from the treasury. Lizzie would email Jo a question, Jo would ask the Treasury, and her status as an MP meant that the Treasury had to respond. These figures were vital in constructing her case for the rise in the threshold. She worked on the details and implications (it would cost £29BN) with the man who had first whispered his displeasure to her in the conference hall.

Much to her own surprise, she found that she was soon in a position to write a policy paper. It was just two sides of A4. The

LibDem womens' network submitted it to the party as a discussion paper for a 'manifesto day' at LSE in January 2009. In the meantime the policy was rejected by her LibDem regional conference for being too expensive.

The LSE day was an overwhelming success. As Lizzie made a speech, she realised that she had a missionary zeal about this policy. During the debate people would say 'You can't do that' or 'If you could do that, someone would have done it already,' but she was undeterred, believing the argument was simple and clear. Suddenly MPs were offering to help her but, in her words, she 'didn't know what to do with them'. With new momentum behind the idea, it was written up as a formal policy motion in June for debate at the main autumn conference – but it would never get there.

In July, Lizzie was coming through the door of her house when she recognised a familiar voice on the TV evening news. Nick Clegg was on screen announcing a £10,000 income tax threshold as official party policy. 'WHAT??????!!!', she thought to herself.

She remembers just standing and staring at her TV from the far side of her living room. She couldn't believe her little idea had come so far, and developed a life of its own! She was over the moon, but never thought for a second that it would be enacted into law. There was not a great history of Liberal Democrat policies ever becoming law. It wasn't the full £11,137 that she had proposed, but it was a huge step in that direction, and more than she would ever have imagined possible.

Then in the days that followed the 2010 election Lizzie was actually distraught to hear about the Conservative/LibDem coalition. 'I didn't want to go in with that lot. But I guess there was no alternative.' One of her main reasons was that she felt David Cameron had been condescending about her idea. She says she often watches a Youtube clip from one of the TV debates where David Cameron says, 'It's a lovely idea Nick, but we just can't afford it.'

Lizzie presumed her policy would never see the light of day in a coalition with the Conservatives, but she was encouraged when she heard that the Income Tax Threshold increase had become a non-negotiable part of the LibDem coalition deal negotiations. There seemed to be favour on her idea from on high. It was agreed.

Lizzie only accepted that her idea was to become reality when she heard George Osborne announce the measure. The level was to be raised in increments so even then she did not believe it would ever actually get to £10,000, but as of 5th April 2014 the Income Tax Threshold has been exactly £10,000.

She says it has been the most amazing feeling knowing that you have made a tangible difference for millions of people. Since then both Vince Cable and Nick Clegg have come back to her to say thank you, with Nick confessing that he now preferred her policy to his original idea. She greatly enjoyed a photoshoot at Big Ben with Tim Farron, the LibDem president, and fellow believer.

The main thing I learned from Lizzie's story was that her long-term involvement in the party gave her many things without which her idea would have remained just that – an idea. These include:

- Her understanding of the struggles of ordinary people, drawn from her local political work.
- Her relationships with people in the party, which allowed her to access resources and wisdom.
- Her knowledge of the processes by which policy could make progress towards being accepted.
- But more than anything it was wonderful that her long-term service to the party meant that she got a fair hearing when she spoke up.

The point here is not so much the policy. You may or may not have a strong opinion on the Income Tax threshold. You may have never heard of it until now. There were Christians on either side of that discussion. The point is that the idea of a 'normal' believer became legislation. It is possible. In a bureaucratic and complicated world, politics still does allow this type of story. Why can't the next story be yours?

Raising the threshold further has now been adopted as policy by the Conservative, Labour and Liberal Democrat parties, so Lizzie's work truly has created a new landscape for this issue.

Lizzie's idea would have remained an idea if it wasn't for her willingness to prepare papers and make her case in meetings. Which leads us neatly onto another major reason why Christians often don't get politically involved.

8

BUT THOSE MEETINGS ARE SO BORING

What? You mean discussing which was the best form of Trotskyism with four senior citizens in a cold, dusty community hall, and arguing over whether there are enough members present to re-elect the treasurer, who presides over a turnover of £37.42, for the seventeenth time, isn't your idea of a fun night out? You mean listening to Brenda complain about the state of the footpaths on Hindman Street since the gas company tore them up doesn't fill you with joy? You mean hearing how the War Memorial service may need to be changed from a Thursday to a Friday because Cyril at the council has had a knee replacement doesn't make you want to blog about it? Hmmph! Kids these days!

As Lizzie Jewkes would probably confirm, actually it's a fair cop. You are correct. Local political meetings can be the equivalent of watching paint dry on someone's nails as they are scraped across a blackboard. A culture of bureaucracy has developed so that it is more important to do everything by the book than to actually get anything done. More worryingly, these processes can serve to exclude those who don't understand what is going on and limit the involvement of new blood. I am really selling it to you, aren't I? Thankfully the stereotyped cliché is much worse than what is increasingly the reality. The influence of community organising methods and church cell-group thinking have started to improve local meetings. But I should not sugar coat it for you. These are the places where it is probably least fun, but often very important to 'show up'.

The thing is, Jesus never called us to comfortable situations, where there were always soft seats, a welcome team and ever-flowing fairly-traded coffee. He mentioned something about taking up a cross, which sounds a bit like hard work. He mentioned something about persistent prayer. And he didn't just talk about it. He fleshed it out in his life. Obedience to his Father and his call always came before comfort or expediency.

Playing our part in society – being citizens rather than mere consumers – is probably harder than spending each evening selecting our next entertainment option or meeting with likeminded believers. But it is ultimately much more fulfilling, and can connect us to God's bigger mission out beyond the walls of the church.

As Christians we are used to meetings. We are used to thinking about team as well as task and can bring a relational edge to meetings which might not otherwise be there. We are also used to turning up on time (roughly) and doing what we say we'll do before the next meeting. Believe me, if you turn up to these gatherings bringing some of these values and carrying even a shred of optimism, enthusiasm and creativity you will find yourself straightaway in the top 5% of local political operatives. You will be offered roles and responsibilities very quickly. I have seen it happen time and time again. Local party memberships are dwindling and often apathetic. Someone who offers even a few encouraging words to those involved sticks out like a sore thumb. Then suddenly you are the chairperson or secretary, with the ability to inspire and shape what is going on. Things may not stay boring for much longer. The opportunities are huge. What happened to Gavin and his friends in Luton is an excellent example.

Revolutions are possible. There are pockets of life all over the country where Christians are getting involved and it is changing the face of dreary local politics. I often challenge the people who co-ordinate how the parties operate around the country with the reality that if you have a 28-year-old who is passionate about justice, and they have just one night free in the week, what will they choose to do? Will they befriend and mentor local young people through the youth club at the local church, will they join an Amnesty group and make campaigning phone calls on various causes, will they volunteer in the local foodbank, or will they sit in a dusty hall agreeing the last meetings' minutes and debating whether Clause 6 or Clause 7 of the local healthcare amenities bill will have detrimental effect on service provision in that ward? The answer is pretty clear. Until politics is also seen as action and service, we will not attract those who are passionate about their communities. It's not that those discussions aren't important. It's just that they need to also be linked to real people through active service.

Here is the pivotal role that Christians can play. As meetings discuss the particular challenges in an area, we are often able to give the best insight into why people are struggling, because the church is rolling up its sleeves and getting involved with some of the most troubled families. Through youthwork, toddler groups, foodbanks, drug rehabilitation programmes, elderly befriending schemes and debt counselling centres, the Christians are often best placed to comment on what the priorities should be in any given area. There is real insight to what programmes or legislation are required by a council. Often others will have anecdotal evidence, but there is a body of evidence that the church is accruing that is hard to ignore. The problem is that in most situations the church is getting on with this great stuff, but no one from the church is sitting in the political meetings telling those stories. Sadly they are two separate worlds, leading to the misunderstandings and miscommunication we often complain about.

I am privileged to receive phone calls and emails from people who I have directly or indirectly encouraged to get involved. A fair summary of those conversations would be something like this:

ME: *'So how did it go?'*
NEW RECRUIT: *'Well it was exactly as you said.'*
ME, NERVOUSLY: *'What do you mean?'*

NR: 'It was incredibly dull.'

ME: 'Ah. Yes they can be.'

NR: 'It was awkward, stilted, and weighed down by bureaucracy.'

ME: 'Just like church then?'

NR: 'Ha, ha. There were a couple of egos competing to be top dog.'

ME: 'Oh, so nothing like church then! (nervous laugh) It is often the way sadly. Even the smallest groups often have factions.'

NR: 'Then they mentioned that they were looking for volunteers to work with young people especially. They couldn't believe we already had so many amazing connections with schools and young people.' (or insert any other demographic)

ME: 'Great'

NR: 'They seemed really impressed with what I shared. They didn't know about a lot of the stuff we've been doing.'

ME: 'Great! A kingdom connection has been made!'

NR: 'Yes, so I've been voted on to the committee!'

ME: 'Brilliant! – well played!'

NR: 'And one of the other members came up to me after the meeting and whispered to me that he was a Christian too.'

The hard sell

There has been a tendency over the last few years for folks like me to sell their particular ministry at events and festivals. The pitch encourages people to get involved because their faith will be stretched, they will experience God's love in action, and they will make their life count. All those things could be true of getting involved in politics, but I also want to tell you the honest truth. Generally people are trying to convince you that you should be doing the same thing that they are doing. It's amazing how we suddenly believe that everyone should be doing what we are doing. Self-justification is a wonderful thing. So I don't know that you should be doing what I'm doing – that's for you and God to sort out – and in fact, here is a warning.

It will be incredibly hard work. It may be incredibly dull work. My old boss Alun Michael MP used to say, 'No matter how high you rise in politics, you are only five minutes away from having to stuff hundreds of envelopes.' I have experienced this to be true many times! Politics is a subculture like any other, and you have to spend time learning the language and building relationships. That is, presuming you want to do it in a relational way. Sadly many Christians choose the instant hit version of political engagement. We want results now. We want action now. So we blunder in like bulls in a china shop without even stopping to ask anyone else why they may hold an opinion different to ours.

There is almost always a story behind the story. Building relationships is inevitably a messier and longer-term strategy. The question you have to ask is are we seeking to persuade actual people of the ways of Christ, or impose his ways on those who may reject him. Surely we want people to desire him and his ways, not simply follow them out of duty. Granted his just ways build a healthy culture and society, but is the prize of persuading someone of his love for them too large to give up? When someone is commanded, they tend to be defensive. When someone is persuaded, they may become disciples. Yes we must stand up strongly on points of principle, but there is a huge difference to speaking truth in love at close range and shouting it from a distance. We all know this from our own close relationships. How do you modify the behaviour of a friend when they are acting in a way that is hurtful to others and to themselves? You speak the truth in love. That may need an arm around the shoulder, or a face-to-face challenge, but you rarely shout from a distance. That doesn't tend to get the best reaction.

Another selling point

There will also be plenty of people lining up to oppose you. And they won't necessarily choose the relational route. Much of the discussion in the twenty-first century public square happens online. I accept that it is possible to build real relationships online, but the vast majority of interaction is distinctly un-relational. Well-known political bloggers hide behind pseudonyms rendering relationship-building even more difficult. People say things to others online that they would not dream of saying to someone's face. We must not retreat from the twenty-first century Areopagus that is Twitter, but we must do it differently to the world. That will mean not responding as fast as we would like, potentially looking silly for a few hours, as we pray and consider a response, rather than knee-jerking. That may mean direct messaging someone or calling them, rather than critiquing them in public. That may mean having Sabbath days when we don't go anywhere near social media, to make sure we are drawing from deeper wisdom, rather than just the shallowness of 'now'.

Service

Can we imagine a better future, where we lead the way in the transformation of both what it means, and importantly the perception of what it means to be involved in local politics? Imagine twenty years from now, a situation where members join to become involved in local teams that serve their communities in practical ways. In the midst of these actions they get to know a much wider spread of the local community, and become known as those that do rather than those that merely come after people when they want their vote. In this future, it is known that folks get into politics to serve their communities rather than gain positions of influence.

The challenge of reconnecting citizen and state is enormous. To begin with, we must understand the perception of the roles of citizen and state in the twenty-first century. As we touched on earlier, in an age of selfish consumerism, reality TV and unbridled choice, when people read 'connections between citizen and state', they subliminally assume you mean mechanisms to help them communicate better what they want the state to do for them. They assume a connection going in only one direction. We need mechanisms to make a two-way street tangible. We need easily accessible ways for citizens to give to their local communities but for these efforts to not be separate from politics. We have seen this happen effectively through projects in places like Warrington, Gosport, Liverpool and Manchester. Teams of political folks have been sweeping streets, litter-picking in parks, cleaning playgrounds, removing needles and building low-cost housing. These projects will only be sustainable if people are working together in teams. These service teams can work in partnership with local voluntary agencies, but be clear about their connection to the wider political discussion. This provides a tangible link between 'politics' and 'local service'.

This is an unashamed attempt to bring the word 'service' properly back into the national and local lexicon. There is a media-led expectation of how we should be served, but fewer frameworks for how people can serve.

One of the knock-on effects of this lack of a mission for citizens is the decline of well-being. Purposeless people are the most disgruntled people. A mission also brings people together in a way that nothing else can. We all know the most meaningful relationships in our lives are those that have been forged while working to achieve a common goal, for example with sports teams or teams that carry out work in developing world contexts.

I believe the results could be healthier, happier, and more integrated communities, for whom it is the norm, not the exception to be 'politically' involved.

This of course is a vision for the future. I cannot claim it is how things are at present. But that does not stop me advocating that you get involved. Many times over the last few years I have reflected upon the 'hierarchy' of sacrifice that subliminally enters the Christian subculture. We applaud those who give up well-paid jobs to go into 'full-time Christian ministry'. We applaud those who go to live in challenging parts of the world. We applaud those who take a stand for what they believe and are persecuted for it. We can visualise these sacrifices of finance, geography and popularity. This leads me to consider each of these sacrifices in my own life. It might sometimes seem easier to raise money when you go to live in a slum than when you pledge to sit in relatively boring meetings. But isn't this also a sacrifice, in an age when we want fast results and to impress each other with photographs on social media of our colourful exploits? Could we carry the cross of the hard yards of nameless, faceless discussions that actually power our country? Or do we instead crave the need to make an impact? And when we say 'make an impact' do we mean 'do lots of stuff and get noticed while we are doing it'? I say this only because I see this unhealthy desire in myself. Is it possible to just be present to the moment without having to share it on social media? Is it possible to perform an act of selfless kindness without blogging about it the next day? Is it possible as Jesus said to 'not let your left hand know what your right hand is doing'? My fear is that after my right hand has done something admirable I now need to use my left hand to click a mouse and tell the internet.

As someone who runs an organisation I understand the need to advertise what we are doing in an attempt to draw more people to be involved. But have we created a culture where the cart is getting before horse? Scripture applauds those whose work is done in secret. We are warned 'Do not despise these small beginnings' (Zechariah 4:10, NLT). We are told that the kingdom of God is 'like a mustard seed' (Mark 4:31), the smallest of seeds, which grows to become the largest of plants. Our kingdom activities will bear fruit in time, but only if we remain in him. Could we be attracted to missional work where there may not be any exciting stories to stand up and share with our congregation for many years? Where there may be no exciting or emotive photographs? Work which won't always be fun because we are working with others who may not have a relational approach to getting work done? Work which will require prayer to bring the life to it, so deepening our faith? Work which will never get us invited to speak at Christian conferences to be heralded by our peers? Work where spreadsheets are about as exciting as it gets?

'Your Father, who sees what is done in secret, will reward you.'

Matthew 6:4b

So far we have listed reasons that Christians don't get involved that are perceptions and sometimes mistaken impressions about politics. Now we turn to a perception about our mission as believers which influences how we think and act with regard to politics.

9

BUT IT'S NOT REALLY A PRIORITY FOR CHRISTIANS IS IT?

If people of faith refuse to participate in politics, then others will make the crucial decisions. In a democracy, the people get the government they choose – and work for. You could say we get the government we deserve. Government can be awful or it can be good; often it is some of both. It is our duty, both as citizens and as Christians, to make it better. The question, then, is not, how can a Christian be in politics? The question is, how can a Christian not be in politics?

Senator Roy Herron

R esponses to our work can often be disappointing. Church leaders will nod, smile and say that it's great that you're politically involved, but that they can't divert any time or resources in that direction. Sometimes this is a practical issue, but more often it is actually a theological issue. There is still a hangover in church culture from a time when we believed that Christianity was solely an escape ticket for a disembodied heaven. If that is true, then of course we won't invest as much time in how we are governed, in caring for the environment or addressing structural injustice. Why would we? Any time spent doing that would inevitably mean less time telling people about their need of Jesus. The argument goes like this: helping the poor is great, in fact, bless you, you are a great example of compassion, but actually what is eternal is more important. I agree. It's just that our understanding of where that eternity is and what it looks like is has shifted dramatically. And I believe it has shifted in a biblical direction.

'Jesus's resurrection is the beginning of God's new project not to snatch people away from earth to heaven but to colonize earth with the life of heaven. That, after all, is what the Lord's Prayer is about.'

Tom Wright, *Surprised by Hope: Rethinking Heaven,*
the Resurrection, and the Mission of the Church
SPCK 2008

It's only too easy to fall into what I sometimes think of as an 'escapology eschatology'. But don't get me wrong – I wholeheartedly believe that individually people need Jesus. Salvation is the heart and centre of our faith. But I also believe the story of the full breadth of that salvation needs telling.

When Jesus encouraged his disciples to pray 'your Kingdom come, your will be done' (Matthew 6:10) he was giving us a clue to what he actually meant every time he spoke of the 'Kingdom of heaven'. When you look carefully at what he said, he could not have been talking about a distant place, about 'pie in the sky when you die'. He was giving the people of the first century images and metaphors to understand what was taking place in front of their eyes, and what continues to happen in front of our rather more sceptical twenty-first century eyes. Yeast, mustard seeds, and fields were telling the story of this incredible kingdom that was being inaugurated through healings, deliverance, the feeding of thousands and words of knowledge.

The work of theologians like Richard Bauckham, Chris Wright and N. T. Wright[1] on this topic is extremely helpful. They speak of our misunderstanding of heaven, which has been based more

---

[1] Dr Richard Bauckham and Trevor Hart, *Hope Against Hope: Christian Eschatology at the Turn of the Millennium* (William B Eerdmans 2009); Christopher Wright, *The Mission of God: Unlocking the Bible's Grand Narrative* (IVP 2006); Tom Wright, *Surprised by Hope: Rethinking Heaven, the Resurrection, and the Mission of the Church* (HarperPaperbacks 2008).

on medieval art and writing (such as Dante) than on Scripture. And there has been a recent surge of interest in heaven – and misunderstanding of it – illustrated by the huge popularity of the *Left Behind* series of novels by Tim Lahaye and Jerry B. Jenkins.

When Jesus speaks of heaven he is speaking of the domain where God's will is always done. This is the sphere of heaven. There is also the sphere of earth, where sadly his will is not exclusively adhered to yet. This makes sense of his prayer – 'your will be done, on earth as it is in heaven' (Matthew 6:10). Think of the famous Mastercard symbol, or any of those Venn diagrams that confused you at school. We experience and pray for moments when heaven touches earth – moments of grace and beauty and compassion and truth, where God's will is done. These are in the intersection of that diagram. One day however these two spheres will be fully fused. The new heavens and new earth combined.

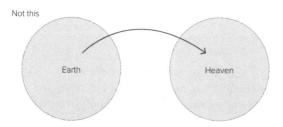

Heaven and earth as separate spheres.

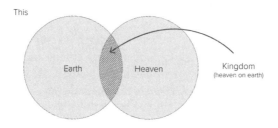

Heaven touching earth: God's kingdom now.

And finally

New heaven and new earth

God's kingdom coming: a new heaven and a new earth.

John, in the book of Revelation says this:

> And I saw a new heaven and a new earth: for the first heaven and the first earth were passed away; and there was no more sea.
>
> And I John saw the holy city, new Jerusalem, coming down from God out of heaven, prepared as a bride adorned for her husband.
>
> And I heard a great voice out of heaven saying, Behold, the tabernacle of God is with men, and he will dwell with them, and they shall be his people, and God himself shall be with them, and be their God.
>
> And God shall wipe away all tears from their eyes; and there shall be no more death, neither sorrow, nor crying, neither shall there be any more pain: for the former things are passed away.
>
> And he that sat upon the throne said, Behold, I make all things new.
>
> Revelation 21:1–5, KJV 2000

This is patently about God making his home here with us, rather than us escaping to some other place. This place will be restored, redeemed and reconciled to its Creator, throughout every dimension of human life. We don't get to choose which things are important according to our perspective or particular passion. He did not say 'I make some things new'. All things will be made new. This passage in Revelation simply echoes the reality of this restoration that has been promised in many other places in Scripture including Isaiah and Paul's letters.

The Greek word for 'new' used here implies re-creation, rather than creation from scratch. It is *kainos*, which Mounce[1] suggests should be understood as 'fresh life rising from the decay and wreck of the old world'. It speaks of the earth being renewed rather than re-created *ex nihilo*. This sits in congruence with the manner in which Jesus was raised from the dead. His new body was different, but in continuity with the his old one. Blanchard says, 'the new body is not identical but will be identifiable with it'.[2]

The verb which we read as 'passed away' in verse 1 is *aperchomai* meaning 'to depart, go away.' The sense here in the context of John's vision is that the old earth has not been incinerated but simply disappeared from his sight. Theologian Gale Heide feels the most important point is that, 'John is not saying that God has simply wiped everything away to begin again with nothing'.[3] John Blanchard backs this up: 'if God were to annihilate the first cosmos and start again, it would at least suggest that Satan had ruined the first beyond remedy.' This is the return to how things were always meant to be. This means from minute individual decisions to huge ecosystems, they will all be transformed to operate in the way that God first intended. In perfection with him for eternity. I cannot wait.

> New creation is precisely that future of the present world, of all created reality, which does not emerge from the history of this world but will be given to it by God. It requires an originating act of God, just as creation in the beginning did, but in this case it will be an act which preserves the identity of the first creation while creatively transforming it.
>
> Bauckham and Hart, *Hope against Hope*

---

[1] William D. Mounce, *Mounce's Complete Expository Dictionary of Old and New Testament Words* (Zondervan 2006).

[2] John Blanchard, 'Whatever Happened to Heaven?' in *Reformation and Revival: A Quarterly Journal for Church Leadership* (Vol 6, No 2) (Spring 1997).

[3] Gale Z. Heide, 'What is new about the New Heaven and the New Earth? A theology of creation from Revelation 21 and 2 Peter 3', in *Journal of the Evangelical Theological Society* (March 1997).

However, we should not lapse into the lazy reactive theology that complains 'The church is obsessed with private morality – we should be talking about justice more' or 'We should be more concerned with the structures of the world than internal salvation'. We need both/and rather than either/or. Salvation is wonderfully real. There is no transformation like the transformation that Jesus Christ brings to a life. Our problem is that we have allowed this transformation to stop at the boundaries of our individual lives.

> The Son is the image of the invisible God, the firstborn over all creation. For in him *all things* were created: things in heaven and on earth, visible and invisible, whether thrones or powers or rulers or authorities; *all things* have been created through him and for him. He is before *all things*, and in him *all things* hold together. And he is the head of the body, the church; he is the beginning and the firstborn from among the dead, so that in *everything* he might have the supremacy. For God was pleased to have all his fullness dwell in him, and through him to reconcile to himself all things, whether things on earth or things in heaven, by making peace through his blood, shed on the cross.
>
> Colossians 1:15–20 (italics mine)

'All things' includes every aspect of creation. God's desire has always been for every sphere of culture to be transformed. Business, Media, Education, Arts, Religion, Family, and even Politics.

We may love the abstract idea of the new heavens and the new earth as future hope. What is sometimes more challenging is to shrink that down to our level. If there is to be a new earth fused with the new heavens then that means there will be a new London, a new Bradford, a new Milton Keynes, a new Inverness. What would a new version of your town, village or city look like? How would the restored, perfected version operate? It is a tantalising thought, but one which also inspires us to be part of demonstrating that future perfection in the now. Why not try it with your church? Brainstorm what your area would look like in its restored version. What would be no more? What would have arrived? These visions can often give us clarity in what we should be working on at the moment. And they make it clear why political engagement will be necessary to see their fulfilment.

Ridiculously, we are called to be partners with God in his mission to see the restoration, redemption and reconciliation of all things. If that is the ultimate goal, then suddenly our involvement in all the structures of this world starts to make sense.

> Therefore, my dear brothers, stand firm. Let nothing move you. Always give yourselves fully to the work of the Lord, because you know that your labour in the Lord is not in vain.
>
> 1 Corinthians 15:58

Can you see how motivating that is? Our efforts are not wasted. Every effort to choose kindness over cynicism, to choose truth over expediency, to choose co-operation rather than competition, to choose love over apathy, makes a mark on the map of forever.

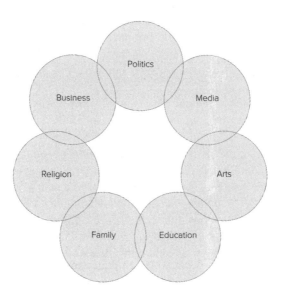

Inhabiting the spheres

So if we are asked to be partners in the transformation of all of life, what might that practically mean?

Social scientists talk of the presence of seven broad areas of life that influence culture. There are small differences between different schemas, but they mostly coalesce around seven areas: government, religion, business, education, family, media, and the arts. These are the areas that have been shown to have the most profound influence on how we think and how we live, forming our culture. Forces and movements from within these areas combine to create the atmosphere of what seems right and wrong, what is acceptable and unacceptable, and where our priorities lie as human beings. These are not insignificant things.

It follows from our eschatology (the description of the new earth mentioned earlier) that if we desire to see the redemption, restoration and reconciliation of all things to their Creator, then we must desire to see the transformation of every sphere of society.

The problem for us as the church is that we have desired that change in the various spheres, but have not always been meaningfully present in those spheres. We have sought change via prayer and petitioning from the outside, but have not always followed Christ's pattern of incarnation by being involved on the inside.

Something that the church leaders I meet will readily confess to is that much of our investment and time in the last thirty years or so has been spent impacting the religious sphere. Our energy and finances have mostly gone into training people to be better worship leaders, better preachers, or better small group leaders. We haven't been investing so much time in training people to be better journalists, better politicians, or better artists. We invest heavily in making our religious 'product' better, most significantly our Sunday gatherings. But if we are investing primarily in the religious sphere, then in theory we may be only impacting one seventh of culture. The church has been waking up to this problem, but sometimes the framing for our endorsement of these jobs in the spheres has been purely evangelistic. Just this year I was at a missionary conference where it was suggested by the main speaker that the only reason Christians should be involved in these spheres was that it would provide a way to meet people who might become Christians. Presence there was just a strategy for saving their souls, rather than a desire to see transformation in each of the spheres. And yes, of course as we disciple people in the religious sphere, we hope that they have more impact in their working environments, but that's not the same as training them up for the specific challenges found within each sphere.

The gospel grinds up against principalities and powers in every sphere, including the religious sphere. There are different challenges in each one, and specific theological work is needed in each sphere. In my particular sphere this has taken the form of some incredible work in political theology from people like Oliver O'Donovan, Jonathan Chaplin, Anna Rowlands and David Landrum, some of which we will cover later in the book. This work provides a spine for those who are getting involved so that they are not blown by the wind once they are involved in the rough and tumble that is politics. Recent history is strewn with too many believers who have attempted to influence a sphere but have not had any brothers and sisters for support and accountability, or anyone doing the hard thinking that is required. Sadly I know too many broken marriages and dreams as a result of this naïvety.

For example in education, how do you demonstrate the kingdom when you disagree with the ideological foundations of something you are being asked to teach? In business, how do you ensure that your supply chains are ethical? In the media, how do you justify working on a production that adds to the shallowness of society? In the arts, how do you tell good stories to a cynical world? In politics, how do you avoid compromise when you are being whipped to vote? In finance, how do you work for an entity that is part of a global system that is making the rich richer and poor poorer?

The lack of an undergirding kingdom eschatology explains so much of our previous political engagement as believers. Without a desire to see the transformation of all things in all spheres of life, our interests were understandably focused on the religious sphere. So we were only politically awoken when someone came to step onto our turf, to disrupt what was going on in 'our world'. So when Sunday trading laws were proposed, marriage was being tampered with, or religious liberty is at stake, then suddenly we were interested. That limited our voice into the rest of the spheres but also allowed us to be characterised as people who only cared about our own issues. It also led to a rather defensive posture and siege mentality spilling out in the tone and methods we used to communicate. Sadly both in the West and in other parts of the world this is still true. We look like those who are rather desperately defending our patch of land, rather than seeking kingdom values in all of society.

So how do you demonstrate the kingdom in the spheres? For too long we have settled for the easy answer of 'just by doing your job well'. This answer is blind to the reality of our fallen world, and fallen structures. We cannot enter spheres in blind faith to their goodness. For example, we would probably not advocate a Christian shining in the brothel industry by just 'doing it really well'. 'Just doing it really well' in the banking and financial industry of the nineties and early noughties was hardly a high enough benchmark. We need to be able to grapple with the tough issues, and not simply assimilate. This assimilation is often subconscious, as each of the spheres comes with an impressive 'enculturation' programme which gradually normalises you to certain practices. People often serve their time as apprentices or interns, during which time they do not feel able to question the conventional practices or wisdom of the sphere. Before you know it, you have been enculturated. Our training of our people needs to start as they enter these spheres, if not before.

'Building' the church

Even when we do appreciate the importance of seeing trans-formation in each of these spheres, we often drag the folks who are working in them back into the religious sphere of church. We employ people in voluntary service to the extent that they have no free time in their week. People can seemingly be at a church building with justifiable reason nearly every night of the week. Those who have some skill in organising or communication (often honed by their work in the spheres) are snapped up and asked to perform various church-based roles, running prayer rotas, worship teams, building committees etc. Of course we should all be willing to serve to make church community life sustainable, but to me it feels like we may have gone too far.

People are left with no time to dwell in their sphere, to build the relationships with not-yet-believers that are crucial to kingdom change. For me this means having time to be able to go to the local branch meetings of the Labour party. When I am having to miss those for another meeting to discuss the worship rota, I know the balance may be sliding the wrong way.

I like the idea of people tithing their gifts towards their local congregation. Enough to serve and build the body, but not so much that they have no time or energy to inhabit their sphere. The temptation of some churches is to grab the talents of artistic people and use their skills to put on the best show possible. It is done with great sincerity, but it can lead to hiding giftings away in the religious sphere. There is a desire for excellence and a desire to be attractive to not-yet-believers. But it breaks my heart when I ask amazing musicians where they mostly play their music and they say, 'Well, mostly in church'. Some may say that is offering your gift back to God (and this is what some are called to exclusively), but I would say there is a danger of too many people hiding their gifts within the walls of the church. I will never forget a church leader saying, when I questioned him about their church's big theatrical productions, that the reason for doing it was 'So that our church is known for its excellence in the town.' I don't think that's a kingdom attitude. That's simply competing to be the best show in town and to attract the most people.

Of course the opposite problem can also arise. Our church decided to put more of our efforts into supporting actors (we had a lot of them) as they made progress in the world of acting. We would go along to their shows, pray for them, and make rehearsal space available. But we started to run into problems when we suggested that they do even small little pieces of theatrical work for gatherings – a dramatic reading, or a monologue. The responses came back, 'Eh, it's not really what I do', or 'Well, theatre is meant to be long form, and it compromises the art', or 'I don't do Christian drama – it's twee', or 'That would be prostituting my art'. Now I understand each of those statements, I wasn't exactly doing the 'art' – in the strictest sense of the word – on a Sunday morning either. I wouldn't call playing repetitive, soft acoustic rock songs in the same key for twenty minutes 'art'. But there has to be some compromise of 'my art' in the cause of finding some common ground to help the whole community worship. So we obviously need a balance, but on the whole it feels as if we in the church need to be 'releasing and supporting' more than 'grabbing and using' our people, whether we are talking about music or politics.

Training

Could we challenge our churches, or groups of churches together in a town, to be providing more support for those operating in the spheres? Could we release and support the entrepreneurs within these spheres to launch and sustain more initiatives like Artisan (for Christians in the arts), Christians in Politics (obvious), Transforming business (for the business world) and Medianet (for Christians in the media)? Could we set about the challenge of not just growing more churchgoers but growing citizens of the kingdom?

At its heart this is a discipleship issue. An average vicar from East London is unlikely to know enough about investment banking, for example, to be able to hold their church member who works for an investment bank accountable in any meaningful way. They are unlikely to be able to ask the right questions to deduce if they are being true to kingdom values. Yes they know that she is a good mother, helps with the church accounts and gives plenty of cash, but during the bulk of her week, is her work glorifying God? The head of pastoral ministry in a West Country church is unlikely to know whether or not the member of their congregation who is involved in modelling is staying true to his faith in the complexity of that world.

Firstly they are not there, sharing the same space, observing their working lives. Perhaps a 'Bring your pastor to work' day would be a good idea. But it is also impossible to get your head around the complex challenges of different environments and cultures. Every culture has its glories and blind spots. Sometimes they can be spotted from outside, but sometimes insider knowledge is required to see how a structure, process or concept could be transformed to be more in line with God's kingdom. That is why vocational groups involving people who are passionate about the different spheres are essential if we are truly to see transformation in these spheres. There is some theological grappling to be done to bring kingdom transformation in every sphere. Answers are rarely clear cut. At what point does a business cease to be ethical? At what point is a council being compliant in an oppressive system? At what point should a doctor withdraw treatment? None of these questions are easily answered, and we need Christians interacting with theologians and other specialists who are focusing on these worlds. These same Christians also need to be attentive to the Spirit as situations unfold. Wisdom is required to translate biblical truth into biblical living as technology progresses and situations change.

Integrity in each of the spheres is so much more than not doing anything illegal and not having an affair. To read some Christian books, you would think that that was the sum total of being salt and light in the workplace. What we desire is transformation – we want to see his kingdom come and his will be done in education, in business, in wherever, as it is in heaven. We want to be at the forefront of better ways of making things happen, not just Christians doing what the world does, but just doing it a bit more nicely.

Greg Valerio is a great example of this happening. He worked in the world of jewellery. He was outraged by the widespread exploitation of miners he witnessed in Africa. But he didn't just campaign against it. He worked to find ways to create an ethical supply chain, and set up the UK's first Fairtrade jewellery company, CRED. He is now at the forefront of enacting change in the industry as a whole. His business was ridiculously small but it has caused a huge sea change. It reminds me of passages like the one in Matthew 13. Here Jesus uses metaphors for the influence of his kingdom which evoke infiltration rather than domination:

> 'The kingdom of heaven is like a mustard seed, which a man took and planted in his field. Though it is the smallest of all seeds, yet when it grows, it is the largest of garden plants and becomes a tree, so that the birds come and perch in its branches.'
> He told them still another parable: 'The kingdom of heaven is like yeast that a woman took and mixed into about thirty kilograms of flour until it worked all through the dough.'
>
> Matthew 13:31–33, NIV

There is a reason I describe the spheres of culture as 'seven spheres' rather than 'seven mountains'. The visual image of a mountain inevitably focuses attention on the top of the mountain, and we spend a lot of time working out how to take the summit. The theory is that if we take the high places of culture, that there will be a kingdom dissemination downwards. Pragmatically I know that this can work, but I think there is a real danger of Christians simply trying to ape the ways of the world. Of course positions of power, be that through wealth, or professional or political status, enable mass reproduction of our thinking and values. History has shown this to be the case. But should this be the unthinking strategy for believers? Of course there are many instances where God calls people to strategic positions – Wilberforce, Daniel, Joseph – but what if our preoccupation with power and celebrity was blinding us to the truth of these verses about the mustard seed and the yeast? Jesus is saying that the kingdom of heaven will not operate via those same top-down power principles. He is speaking about something much more viral. Aiming for the top often means we stop believing that God can do miraculous things through anyone, and we rely on human strategy as the way to transformation. Greg and Lizzie's stories are great examples of yeasty, bottom-up transformation. We need to simply serve locally in politics or business as well as reaching for the stars

For this infiltration of the systems of our world I suggest we need three things, and if one is missing, as I have seen all too painfully in my own life, then we will be much less effective, and potentially ineffective for the kingdom. They are presence, purity and power.

Presence. Being present is crucial for coming to understand and work within a location or sphere. Being there, building a life, means that we are invested, and to some extent dependent on those contexts in which we are placed succeeding.

> Also, seek the peace and prosperity of the city to which I have carried you into exile. Pray to the LORD for it, because if it prospers, you too will prosper.
>
> Jeremiah 29:7, NIV

Purity. Daniel was present in an incredibly dark regime, but his presence brought light. In the midst of it, there was a time to comply and a time to conscientiously object. It will be no different for us. We must maintain our purity to be able to be used as his vessels. Like the people of Israel before us, we cannot divorce our devotional and ethical life from the mission we are called to; they are absolutely bound up together. Who we are must communicate who God is, his nature, his priorities, his love. But we must be there in the midst of businesses, academia, politics, or the media for this to be possible.

Power. Why power, given all we've said about the dangerous pull towards the top of the mountain? Because we need to depend on God's power. We hear too many stories of remarkable miracles and healings happening only in Christian gatherings rather than in any of the other spheres of life. Spiritual gifts are at their sharpest when used out in the marketplace, not within the four walls of a church gathering. This is how kingdom-shaped transformation occurs. The ordinary are given extra-ordinary opportunity and responsibility when they allow God to use them supernaturally. Daniel and Joseph's supernatural dream interpretations spring to mind. Yes, they engaged with the alien culture. Yes, they did their duties to the best of their ability. But if their busy-ness or driven-ness – even from good motivation to be a kingdom influence in high places – had compromisd their tight relationship with God, their presence there would have been little more than making up the numbers. Those moments of God-inspired favour with rulers and others would not have happened. Increasingly I see that this is God's way, as it reminds us that it his mission. I see many Christians involved in politics who work hard, go to all the right meetings, meet all the right people and say all the right things. They are often frustrated when someone else comes along who hasn't done those things, but gets selected to fight a parliamentary seat or gain a promotion within a party. Those hard yards are not a bad idea, in fact they are essential, but if we are disconnected from an openness to the randomness of God's spirit leading and speaking, then we are wasting the opportunities that would come along, burning ourselves out instead, trying to 'make it happen', and forfeiting the joy of his 'easy yoke'.

We must remember that earthly power is not bad or secular. It is in fact God-given as we shall see in our tour through Scripture. It is however much more apparent in its visibility and hence the necessary reminders about God's invisible power!

But what could this look like?

Support and release

So having set the wider context, let's look specifically at government. The sphere of government is not all about politics – there are those involved in the legal professions and the civil service who are crucial to governance, but it is undeniably a strategic area. So how might we meaningfully support those who are involved, rather than just paying lip service to it being a good idea?

There has been an explosion of Christian franchises, if you like, in the last few years. Foodbanks, CAP debt centres, street pastors, and Alpha are just some of the most prominent examples. If you have a bunch of folks who are passionate about young people they can get to together to walk the streets as Street Pastors. If you have bunch of folks passionate about those in debt, you can gather to form a debt centre and so on. Alpha in its very DNA is also about gathering.

The challenge for Christians in Politics meeting locally is that in the final analysis, you want them to be mostly dispersed rather than gathered. On any given Tuesday night, you want Sid to be at the local Conservative branch meeting, Jean to be at the local Labour branch and Sean to be at the local LibDem meeting. You don't want them meeting each other all the time.

So what could local expressions of Christians in Politics groups look like? How could they interest and welcome those who have a passion for their community but don't think that they are 'political' (even though they probably are)!

In any given church there may not be enough Christians who are involved in politics or passionate about politics to form a sustainable support group. But in all the churches of a town or borough, there will be a number of people who could come together to form a critical mass. This is increasingly possible through the improving relationships between churches. This has happened as churches partner together for mission – running foodbanks, co-ordinating youthwork, and providing volunteers to many council-run events – rather than just coming together to have a joint service. The Gather Network and Cinnamon Network are two of the bodies who are helping to support these Churches Together initiatives. So in Southwark, we are meeting together under the banner of 'Transform Southwark (politics)' as others meet as 'Transform Southwark (media)'. Across the churches there are plenty of folks from different backgrounds who are engaged in the spheres in different ways. To meet together brings a sharpening and an accountability. When folks represent different political parties, it means relationships are built that go some way to preventing the lazy stereotyping of 'the other side' when they face each other in the media or at hustings. When people gather, they pray for one another and share honestly about the particular challenges of their roles. Because their peers are also involved in that world, they are able to give knowing, meaningful support and also ask the right questions to hold their friends accountable. Reading the Bible together provides a fabulous plumbline to make sure the members of each camp are not starting to find their identity in their tribe rather than in Christ. The differing interpretations of Scripture remind those present that not everybody necessarily thinks like they do.

This year has also seen the launching of *Restore* groups around the UK. They are based on asking a very simple question, 'What would a restored version of our community look like?' Groups brainstorm this question for twenty minutes, pray for twenty minutes, then plot and scheme for twenty minutes. Some of the answers lead to practical direct action, but many of the conclusions drawn by groups are that they need to be in positions of influence in their local communities to see the sort of transformation they desire taking place. Once you are discussing how to make the seafront a more appealing place, it doesn't take long to realise that some legislation will be required to make that happen in a sustainable way. Resources will have to be apportioned, volunteers rounded up, and new designs contracted. When we look with this sort of long-term view, churches start to see that going to clean up the street for an afternoon is great, but not enough. If the systems don't allow for some ongoing cleaning, then our impact will always be short-term. It may make us feel good about ourselves, and lead to some great pictures in the local paper, but is it bringing long-term sustainable transformation? Politics won't make that happen on its own, but it is surely a large part of the picture.

Again, we are not trying to say that politics is more important than say, prayer, or direct action, in any given community, but that at the moment, there are far less of us doing politics, compared to the other two. Could we be part of that changing? It is important however not to be lulled into a utilitarian gospel that is all about sorting out the world. Public leadership transcends just 'sorting things out'. Leadership in the public square does shape culture for better or worse, either creating or shutting down the space for certain strands of thought and action. It has an influence on the personal and spiritual realm too. When we abdicate ourselves from that sort of leadership we allow those who would wish to operate from a utilitarian mindset to dominate the imaginations of people. We will be left with no defence against the de facto definition of humans as economic units and the ensuing exploitation, consumerism and individualism.

Or, we could show up.

Congruent flow into the media

The spheres of culture are not separate, but continually interweaving. You don't have to be a genius to spot that the relationship between politics and the media is a crucial one. This has always been the case, but has become even more so in the last two decades, as twenty-four hour news media and the internet have come to dominate public discourse.

Sadly political parties are spending much more on employing people to manage the message than they are on people who will actually work on policy. To say the media is all-powerful is an exaggeration, but it is not far from the truth. This is even more concerning when you note that in the world of the media, money talks. Newspapers, websites and magazines are often owned by people who have a particular outlook on life, and inevitably their media outlets are steered to favour stories and reporting that will substantiate that worldview. We need to bear this in mind when we engage with any sort of media. The increasing consumerisation that we have spoken about before also applies to our consumption of media. Rather than engage with it critically we often simply engorge it, presuming anything and everything we read or see is unfiltered truth.

I have seen too many believers step into strategic roles with great enthusiasm, only to be ground down by how their efforts are reported in the media. This was especially true of believers who were elected to parliament in the 1997 General Election. Quite a few of them confided to me that they came into parliament on a wave of passion to 'make a difference'. However this enthusiasm was quickly muted when they were taken aback by press stories about their work or their personal lives. They rapidly recalibrated their work to a pattern of keeping their heads down to maintain a quiet life. Until you have experienced the intensity of negative stories in the press about you it is hard to imagine the constant stress it causes. You are aware in every conversation you have that the person you are speaking to may well have read that particular story and that their opinion of you may have been tainted. You feel the need to explain or apologise or set the record straight continually. It is exhausting. Either that or you develop a cold heart that becomes unaffected by these darts. Sadly that is the route many go down, and it leads to the lack of humanity politicians are, ironically, pilloried for. We are working with our future candidates to ensure that they can develop and maintain a thick skin but a soft heart.

But there is another more profound reason why Christians often fare badly in the press. There is a chronic lack of relationship between Christians and those in the mainstream media. When an article in *The Independent* or *The Daily Mail* makes you want to scream, 'But that's a crazy misrepresentation of the church', stop for a moment to consider why that may be true. If the journalists writing those pieces even had fleeting real relationships with believers, or even better worked with them, they would not be able to get away with writing what they write. Often we simply aren't there. We have left that job to someone else. Christian writers are often writing for Christian magazines and blogs rather than mainstream newspapers. Our friends in Christians in Journalism, Medianet and the Churches Media Council do a great job of encouraging the flow in the right direction, but they suffer from the same lack of resources as Christians in Politics. As the church, we have not had always had a strategy of integration, but one of separation.

That is why alongside a new wave of Christians entering party politics, we need a congruent flow of Christians getting involved in journalism and other areas of the media. Simply by their presence certain ways of writing and easy presumptions are stalled. I know that the presence of Christians on the Left in Labour HQ, where we are based, has meant things have been said or done differently than if we were out of sight and out of mind. We need strategic relationships between those in the media and politics, to allow the communication of better narratives than those we have at present. We are naïve to think that just because what we are saying is true that it will somehow find its way to the ears of the nation.

Final thoughts

So in closing this chapter, I am not claiming that politics is the most important sphere in which we long to see the present expression of its future, final transformation. But it is surely one of the most strategic. God's kingdom is a story of infiltration not domination. His power is used to release people into true freedom rather than control them. We engage in politics not because it controls all of life, but because along with the arts, media, education, family, religion and business it creates the culture in which we live and breathe. In fact a large part of what we as Christians bring to politics is some perspective on the limitations of politics. There is only so much transformation that can be wrought from the 'external' work of politics. That is not to say internal and external do not interact (as we have already discussed) but that the externalities of life which politics control only tell a portion of the story of our lives. My neighbours' lives will be better because they have better healthcare provision, freedom to worship whom they choose, benefits when they are unable to work, and police to protect them from burglary, but they will also be better if they believe the truth about who God is and who he has made them to be, and if they are living in healthy relationship to him and their neighbours. Politics can make some impact, but it is far from total. We pray and work simultaneously because we believe the battles are both visible and invisible.

There is always a temptation in any line of work to see the world through the lens of what you do day in day out. We see issues as primarily economic, artistic, or familial, dependent on our expertise. As Christians in Politics we are able to point out to politicians that some problems require more than political solutions. The offer to pray in political contexts is often a surprise to people, but often well received.

There are also many functional arguments for political engagement that could be made at this point based on solid biblical scholarship. By that I mean that it seems foolhardy to try to follow the biblical injunctions to care for the widow or the alien without setting up some systems to allow you to. The Bible is certainly not only advocating random compassionate charitable responses when we stumble upon need. Scripture after Scripture makes it clear that a more structured approach is required. Here we think of Jubilee, Sabbath, many other Old Testament regulations and the rhythms of the early church. Or to properly follow the commands to care for creation, it similarly seems ridiculous to follow them as individuals alone. We will be handicapped in our attempts to live well if we are all left to our own devices.

So we can make functional arguments for why we need politics to fully flesh out God's heart for his creation, but what we have been saying is something more profound than that. God actually cares about governance. He is passionate about the means as much as the ends.

It is also worth noting at this point another reason why we cannot leave politics in the functional part of our brains. For many politics is a vocation, a holy calling to serve in a specific field of life. This specific calling is an echo of the calling we all have, or more accurately, the identity we all have as kings and priests. We are speaking a lot in this section about the glory of God's perfect future, but we are not mere spectators either in the present or the future. Scripture tells us that we will be kings and priests reigning with God over his restored creation. Surely to live with integrity now in light of that future is to practise both those priestly and kingly roles. We often speak of learning to worship now, because it's what we'll be doing for ever, but that misses a huge chunk of the story. It is promised that we will be sharing the joy of managing this perfection. Our tendency as humans is to keep life incorrectly simple, focusing on one or other of these two roles. We either major on being priests, with our focus on spiritual things, or major on being kings with our focus on practical things. It is not the church's job to be a spiritual service provider when the nation needs a conscience, funeral or a wedding, leaving all the governing to the practical folks. This is not the vision of Scripture. But this is sadly the post-Christendom, post-modern hand we have been dealt, where society wishes the church would just get back in its elegant box rather than pester the rest of society with concerns about how we are governed and how we live together.

Elizabeth Berridge is someone for whom this properly integrated thinking has become reality. We hear her story next.

10

SHOWING UP:
ELIZABETH BERRIDGE

L et me tell you about Elizabeth. She describes herself as an ordinary girl, growing up in an ordinary market town, going to an ordinary church. A trip to the cinema required a considerable journey and her life horizons were relatively near. Her family weren't churchgoers and none of them had been to university before. Her mum and dad met while working in the local plastics factory. The demographic make-up of her town was mostly white, but for some reason, Elizabeth had always had an interest in Africa and its people.

One Sunday morning in the months before she was preparing to go to university, a visiting preacher suggested she should take a year out with AIM (Africa Inland Mission). She applied and was accepted, but her placement fell through (the first time this had ever happened) and as a last minute fix she applied to YWAM (Youth With a Mission) who placed her in Ghana. It is amazing how lives can pivot on such moments. But for that switch she may not have heard what she needed to hear. Her 'year out' happened in the era before email and mobile phones, and her immersion in Ghanaian culture was total. She called home just twice in nine months.

While in Ghana, she was stretched beyond her comfort zones, serving the local community in a variety of ways, from teaching to decorating to building. The encounter that changed her direction of travel happened in the assembly hall of the local school on the outskirts of Community 13 in Tema. The hall consisted simply of breeze blocks with a corrugated iron roof. Within it sat an old fashioned blackboard on an easel. What was drawn on that board would reshape her life.

The YWAM students were being taught that morning by visiting speaker Landa Cope. Something about being away from her normal context allowed Elizabeth's mind to see things in a fresh way. Landa drew seven circles representing the seven spheres of society – government, business, religion, media, education etc. She explained that like any citizen, Christians should be living out their passions in these public spheres, rather than retreating to their own little caves. She drew that cave on the blackboard too. It had a profound impact on the students. Elizabeth described the experience as 'the electricity being turned on'. She knew from that moment that the sphere of government was where she was called to be. She was pretty sure it was God calling, as there was no political heritage in her family and she wasn't in contact with anyone in that world. It would not have occurred to her naturally. She had a firm conviction from that moment that that was where she would end up, but she had no idea how that could happen, as even the concept of 'being in government' was at that stage beyond her comprehension.

On her return, she did a law degree and then worked as a barrister in Manchester for nine years. At that point she thought she was 'doing government'. Looking back she realises it was good preparation, but that she obviously had a faulty view of constitutional law! She had avoided student politics because she couldn't stand the Union 'talkshop', but politics would come back into focus for her. It happened upon realising that she had no desire to follow either of the prescribed career paths for her profession – to become a QC or a judge. So her passions must have been leading her somewhere else. A friend gave her a leaflet about the Conservative Christian Fellowship which then lay on the floor of her flat for some time. Then one day at a Bar School dinner, a friend (who would go on to be Attorney General) asked her what she believed about politics. She replied that she believed in a small state, including a large voluntary and charitable sector, less centralisation and diligent oversight of government. She added that as a Christian she believed in our corruptible human nature and therefore the need for checks and balances. He replied, 'You're a wet Conservative'. She was a bit shocked as throughout a politics A-level in the mid-1980s she had never thought she was a Tory! Through further conversations her own thoughts crystallised, and the day after the 1997 election she cold-called Conservative Central Office, telling them she wanted to join. They thought it was a hoax. After their biggest defeat of the century, someone was wanting to join? But she did, and has never looked back. Through the Conservative Christian Fellowship she was introduced to members of parliament like Gary Streeter and Caroline Spelman, who spent generous amounts of time with this 'blow-in from the north'. She remembers that there was great value in being with others who were exploring the same avenues that she was.

She stood for election to parliament in 2005 in Stockport, which was, and remained, a very safe Labour seat. She didn't use any of the central Conservative campaign literature because she didn't like it, not realising at the time that that was frowned upon. She enjoyed hustings but found it a bit of a shock when Christians especially were so partisan.

Another trip to Trinidad and Tobago underlined her passion to see injustices addressed and to be a voice for those who are not being heard in any given debate. Elizabeth says she will always spot who is not 'in the room' in a meeting. Having been based in the north-west, it gives her a perspective on how London-centric much media and political discussion is. As she puts it, she got involved in a Conservative party which at that time was very rural and had little understanding of ethnic minorities, especially the British black community. She was appointed as the Director of the Conservative Christian Fellowship and used her position to lobby internally within the party, as they 'really didn't understand this stuff'. She was told she was 'nicely aggressive' in trying to help bridge that education and experience gap. Her history in Africa and the Caribbean gave her authenticity with those communities who were suspicious of Conservatives. Gradually she built up trust and solid links.

During her time in charge there was a transformation of the Under 35s Leadership Programme. More young black people were confident to apply and do the course. Another highlight was reinstituting the party conference church service – a local Methodist church was rammed full of hundreds of people in Bournemouth. She believes God was on the case because the police had messed up many folks' accreditation, so they came to the service while they waited to get into conference! She believes this was a bridgehead moment. Many Conservative MPs didn't see urban life, they only saw rural parish life so it was an eye opener to meet the Tribe of Judah choir from Jesus House.

Elizabeth also put in some hard yards building a relationship with another awkward character – in her words 'a raving socialist' called Andy Flannagan. We disagreed on many things politically, but formed a firm friendship based on our passion to see God's kingdom come on all sides of politics. This led to the re-invigoration of Christians in Politics, which had lain relatively dormant for some years.

We now have increasing numbers of invites to speak at events, conferences, churches and theological colleges. Much of this is down to Elizabeth's foundational work.

I will let Elizabeth tell the next twist of the tale in her own words.

'After the General Election of 2010, a lot of the relationship network I had started out with had got into positions – MPs, special advisors, other roles, and I was still at the Conservative Christian Fellowship. I partly felt 'Gosh I'm not in government, even though my party is in government for the first time since I've joined. Did I get this right?' But then after a rest came a real willingness to carry on with what I was doing in submission. Literally on the very same day that I prayed 'I am going to continue to give this my best', a phone call came out of the blue from the Prime Minister's chief of staff. I don't remember much about the conversation. I was just utterly shocked and blown away and could not comprehend what he was saying to me.'

She was being asked to become a member of the House of Lords. Ironically Elizabeth didn't even know what the system of appointments was, and had recently sent a letter to the chief of staff and the Leader of the House recommending two other people who she thought would be good in the Lords. But never for one second did she think that she would be appointed. Especially as at the time of the call she was thirty-eight. The average age of her new colleagues was seventy-one. If that is not favour from God, I don't know what is.

Since arriving in the Lords, Elizabeth has certainly had an impact. It is often the little things that make a difference even if they do not make the news. She spotted a loophole in the residence tests for Syrian refugees, which was preventing access to legal aid. She has instigated an all-party group on international religious freedom. She has lobbied to amend legislation on 'revenge porn' and raised the profile of the Central African Republic. She has built deep relationships and prays regularly with colleagues from the other parties.

However it has also been sobering for her to see how hard it is to change things. It takes a lot of energy and time to mobilise people even to change a small piece of legislation. There is a lot of work gaining colleagues support and building coalitions. This also requires a lot of admin which she would admit is not her strong suit. She now sees the role as a marathon not a sprint.

I am very proud of my friend, now Baroness Berridge. Her story is testimony to what God can do when someone gives themselves wholeheartedly to his plans and purposes, sacrificing personal gain and comfort for a life in the combative world of politics. I hope that her story makes you believe that it could be true for you too.

As with the House of Commons, the House of Lords can bring forward legislation, but its unique role is the in-depth scrutiny of legislation that originates in the House of Commons. It provides a forum for independent expertise in areas such as Europe, science and technology, economics, communications and the constitution. The decisions of ministers and government departments are questioned and debated. In effect it provides a safety valve to check that there are no unintended consequences to new laws, before they officially become law. Most members of the House of Lords are now nominated by the three main parties, leading to allegations of establishment cronyism. However many also believe that it is important to have some people looking at legislation who have the freedom of not having to always look over their shoulders at public opinion. They can instead focus on what they believe will work, based on many years of wisdom.

11

BUT WE'RE BUSY DOING GREAT STUFF ON OUR OWN

'We are not to simply bandage the wounds of victims beneath the wheels of injustice, but we are to drive a spoke into the wheel itself.'

Dietrich Bonhoeffer, 1939

Increasingly, and understandably, this fifth reason is a major factor. So many churches across the UK are now having a sustained impact on their communities, through working with people rather than doing things to them. Whether it's debt counselling, youth clubs, pregnancy advice centres or foodbanks, God's people are seeking to bring transformation to every aspect of people's lives.

All of this is crucial. But there is a definite temptation. We are often able to see the transformation up close. We are able to connect hand-to-hand and face-to-face. Civil rights leader Martin Luther King once explained that as the church we often enjoy playing the Good Samaritan on life's roadside. We are wired for compassion. It comes naturally. It gives us a sense of significance and an immediate buzz from having tangibly helped. He went on to warn that we rarely take the time to do the harder work of going back to the Jericho road. Who is going back to work out how to stop more people getting mugged? Could we improve the lighting, or increase the policing? Perhaps some more CCTV cameras are needed? The thing is that those are political decisions. But they're often made around dull committee room tables poring over statistics and reports. You know that those small changes will mean hours of potentially boring meetings. But surely that is also where we need to be, bringing salt and light and the drive to make change happen.

Archbishop Desmond Tutu put it like this. 'As Christians, we need to not just be pulling the drowning bodies out of the river. We need to be going upstream to find out who is pushing them in.'[1] As Christians, our compassion makes us very good at treating victims, bringing Christ's care. However we live in the context of a global economic system that is widening the gap between rich and poor. Even the advocates of the unbridled free market admit that the bottom billion of our world cannot even make it onto the ladder, never mind climb up it, with our present system. New victims are being created every day. But as the church we will be stuck treating victims for the next hundred years unless we employ intelligence and leadership to help bring some change to the system. We also need to be involved to make sure that systems don't hold people in dependency, and instead encourage them to take responsibility for their actions.

You see there's a big difference between charity and justice. We enjoy dishing out charity, as it actually makes us feel good. We enjoy helping the struggling family. We feel better because we have given a pound to the beggar. Even if our work is properly empowering people to make better decisions for themselves and could not be pigeonholed as mere charity, it is often hands-on.

Charity is the sticking plaster that is required because injustice remains. Showing compassion deals with the symptoms of a sick global system, whereas seeking justice pursues a cure for the disease with which it is riddled. We often prefer charity to justice because charity makes us look good, but challenging systems involves inevitable conflict with powerful vested interests for whom the present system works very well. These are the prophetic battles that we often back away from as they will involve disagreements with corporations, politicians, or councils.

---

[1] Given in a seminar on Faith and Politics, Johannesburg, January 1989.

At Christians in Politics we often observe people making a journey along a spectrum of engagement. It runs from apathy to charity to justice-seeking.

People are lifted from their apathy by some form of engagement with their local communities. This happened to many Christians during 2008 through the HOPE08 campaign, where over 1,500 villages, towns and cities took part in unified missional efforts in their communities. Through these projects, people were exposed to some of the huge needs in their communities. They saw the challenges for those on limited or no incomes. They saw the difficulties of those with disabilities and those whose family backgrounds militate against self-belief or learning. These interactions left people thinking, 'Why?' Why is the playing field so skewed? What can we do that means that we aren't coming back here every year to do the gardening, or restore the playground? What background issues that leave people in poverty do we need to challenge? Once you start asking these questions, you are inevitably coming up with answers that need political expression. Interestingly, they may also lead you in different political directions, from the same motivational starting point. This is another reason why as Christians we shy away from this part of the process, because we want to avoid conflict with one another. One Christian will see a situation and feel inspired to campaign for a living wage to be paid, while another may see the same situation and campaign for measures to strengthen family life, or free up entrepreneurs to start small businesses.

So could we make this testing part of the journey from charity to justice-seeking? It's not that we leave compassion and charity behind – perhaps a better description of that spectrum would be a spiral where we revisit different areas of engagement as we journey outwards from our selfish self towards God's world.

Speed

Especially in larger, vibrant churches, which are happily bursting at the seams, I hear this sort of narrative from church leaders. 'We are seeing tangible holistic transformation in people's lives through our projects. The engine for them is our dedicated volunteers. They wouldn't be so committed if it wasn't a church programme. The buzz they get from serving and praying on a team with other believers is huge. In contrast the council are incredibly bureaucratic, slow and inefficient. We can deliver results much faster.'

The reality is that churches often spend more time engaged in their own programmes because, if we're honest, they can be faster at making transformation happen. Churches can help people pretty much straight away, and do it without the constraints of people who we may not agree with, or may ask us to fill in a hundred forms. Compare that to how slowly change seems to occur in the political realm. It can take many years for an idea to get from the moment of inspiration to the moment of legislation, and then many more years until it has its impact. But the change that is wrought can influence a whole nation or the world, rather than just a few people. The change may also be longer lasting, as it is not just based on relationships, energy and immediate opportunities. It may reach the parts of the nation that churches don't yet reach. Think of the legislation mentioned earlier to ban smoking or wear seatbelts. Long-term good for public health has been achieved. Culture has been shaped in a huge way. Legislation is not the only thing that can do that, but it can play a very significant part. Surely as Christians we believe that every dimension of human life and culture should be influenced by God's kingdom truth and life. Could we cope with slower change that may last a lot longer?

Of course it's both/and rather than either/or, but again a bird's-eye view of the UK today reveals that there are more Christians involved in transformative hands-on church-based mission projects than in mission that seeks to shape the structural make-up of a village, town, city or nation. Again, do we need to use our resources more strategically? Do we need to let go of the sometimes selfish need to see the transformation in front of our own faces? Could we stop seeing the work as our mission and start trying to find our place in *his* overall mission to see the redemption, reconciliation and restoration of all things?

Local *versus* national

Another hurdle in this area is that our thinking about politics is often constrained by the associations that the word throws up. When we hear the word 'politics' our thoughts turn towards the soap opera in Westminster. Politics is a word that simply describes how we order our relational priorities in the world. It applies just as much to local politics and local communities as to the national picture. Thinking only about the national picture leaves us even more in the place of commentator or consumer, rather than participant. The doors are actually much more open in local politics for believers to have significant influence. It is an opportunity that many churches are missing out on. At Christians in Politics we have discovered at first hand how hard it is to tell the story of local engagement. We have at times made progress with media outlets – magazines, radio and TV stations – in developing regular political slots. But when the content of these slots comes up for discussion, the question always seems to be, 'So which MPs should we get on, and which issues should we discuss?' Yet again the people at home are reduced to the role of commentators rather than potential participants. We give our views on what the expert said, sliding into the cliché of talk-radio. In general not many people hear an MP speaking and think, 'I could do that'. My plea is that instead of that sort of media content we have more empowering stories of local people simply taking the next step on their journey; becoming school governors, becoming local magistrates, joining their local political party. Those things seem achievable and may encourage others in the same direction. But sadly the desire for big names often wins out.

Another problem is that supporting those working in the spheres can be much less satisfying for a church leader. It is much easier to point to a new building, a foodbank, or a youth project and say 'We did that'. It is much harder to quantify and then advertise your work in helping your members have kingdom influence in their spheres. Perhaps no one will ever know that your pastoral words were the difference between someone staying involved in politics and throwing it all in. No one may ever know that you and other members of the leadership team helped a young candidate to deliver their leaflets through 1,500 letterboxes.

In Chapter 17 you can read plenty of examples of Christians who are serving as local councillors.

Vertical and horizontal

I am privileged to attend many Christian events and conferences with two different hats on. I speak at seminars on all things pertaining to worship, and I also speak at plenty of seminars relating to politics. I think you know which seminars get the bigger numbers. It's not even close. My estimate would be in the region of a ratio of ten to one. Don't get me wrong, I am excited that people want to learn about leading their brothers and sisters in worship. I am excited that our orientation is primarily vertical more than horizontal. But it does underline how our churches subliminally prioritise different areas of work.

The opportunities at a local level are huge. If it helps, then don't call it politics. Local political parties are dwindling in their membership, and often drained of any new ideas.

If I had a penny for every after-school club, nursery space, or drop-in centre that has been built in the last twenty years and then had to close again for lack of funding, staff or volunteer support, I would be a fairly rich man. Slowly but surely councils are starting to see that it makes more sense to invest where you already have a ready-made base of volunteers, who have a passion for the elderly of a certain area, or the youth on an estate. Then the facilities and buildings can grow with the life of the project rather than imposing the 'If we build it, they will come' methodology.

Sadly it is common for the church to get on with its work, while statutory agencies get on with their work. There is a distant relationship between people who have considerable shared passion for their communities. In my experience, relationships formed in shared service are strong enough to survive when there are differences in attitudes to policy questions. But when there is little or no relationship there is misunderstanding and conflict. Working together locally can form what some may see as unlikely relationships that tend to bear much fruit for the kingdom.

Local democracy

In 2008 I had the privilege of standing in a by-election for Lambeth council. The ward I was standing for, Vassall, stole a place in my heart. Sitting between Brixton and Camberwell, Vassall contained about 15,000 people, and had some serious problems. You won't find too many people saying that they live in Vassall. For one thing it doesn't really exist. It is a council ward designed for logistical reasons by drawing lines on a map rather than representing a specific community. Until it comes to election time, no one really talks about Vassall as a place, and even then it's probably only the political fanatics.

It boasted more CCTV cameras than the whole of Edinburgh and 36% of the residents had no qualifications of any description. So there weren't a lot of books in the houses and flats we visited, and you can imagine the subterranean levels of aspiration. People here were not being dealt a head start in life. The estate blocks themselves seemed to be designed in such a way as to facilitate crime. I started to think the architects must have been getting a take from the local mafia. There were copious dead ends and dark corners.

I remember my small group praying for me as I pondered whether or not to stand for selection. It would mean a huge commitment of time, and I already had plenty going on. I was also worried I might be eaten up by the party machine and lose the truth of who I was in the process. But something felt incredibly right about taking this step out into the deep water, where I was ill-equipped to swim. Something told me that being in this place where I would need a lot of outside help and a lot of prayer would be ridiculously healthy. From the moment I was selected it was a non-stop adventure of letting locals know who this random Irish boy was. Photographs, biographies and other stories were scattered. I was surprised, yet encouraged that the fact I was a Christian was splashed across the top of the party election leaflets. Then something began to happen that took the Labour party people by surprise. Lots of non-Labour party people started turning up to campaign for me. And not in small numbers – in large numbers. The locals were a bit flabbergasted. They said this never happened. They couldn't understand why folks who weren't party members would bother to come out and campaign. I was able to say, 'I think there is a lot more about church people that you are about to find surprising'. I was so thankful to all the amazing friends, who stood alongside me in that election. It was a truly humbling thing to see people come out night after night to an area they barely knew. The local folks were also a bit shocked by the positive mood – not to mention the amount of food – that the outsiders brought. This was actually starting to be fun. I have never been more proud of the church being church than during that period.

As I wandered around the estates, knocking on doors, I started to realise something else. There weren't too many other people knocking on these peoples' doors. These folks didn't get too many opportunities to tell their stories and feel connected to the big picture. As I listened to their stories, tales of incredible struggles and impressive effort on behalf of their families, I was suddenly very humbled. The honest reality was that someone like me would probably not be knocking those doors unless I was looking for their vote. (At that time I didn't live on an estate.) In a 'Eureka' moment, I experienced the imperfect beauty of democracy, acting like a magnet to bring society at least a little closer together. Before I deigned to represent this area I had to experience to some extent what life was like there. Many people report similar experiences of campaigning. Having at first dreaded the thought of knocking on a stranger's door, they are now energised by these life-giving connections. There aren't too many contexts in modern life where you just meet people as they are.

It struck me what an incredible missional opportunity the church is so often missing out on. The conversations I got into on the doorsteps were incredible. When people haven't had anyone listen to them in a while, it's amazing how they will download so much of their hurt and their heart to you even as a stranger. Of course, you also often had people slamming the door in your face and swearing at you, but it made me think that at last I was experiencing a little bit more of what Jesus meant when he described himself as the scandalon, the rock on which people would stumble, either accepting or rejecting him.

It was inspiring to work with local councillors to help folks get simple things like guttering, bins, heating or playgrounds sorted. I also experienced how thankless the role of a local councillor can be. No thanks for the things you get done, but lots of abuse for the things that you haven't managed to get to, in a role that you are performing in your spare time. It struck me that much of what I saw going on was incredibly Christlike in its humble service.

There were more than a few upsides from fighting that campaign. Sometimes you only really build meaningful relationships when you are working on a team with people, with a shared cause. It cemented many relationships with folks in the party. It meant I connected with some Government ministers who came to campaign with me. I also found a wife. Jenny Grove saw my Facebook requests and decided to come along and help me campaign. I was seriously impressed.

I should point out however that I lost the election. Badly. It wasn't even close. But I had complete peace that I had walked the right path in doing it. Without that experience, there is no way I could do the job I do now, encouraging others to do the same. There are dynamics and motivations that you can only really experience from the inside. Also if I had won, there is no way I would have the time to do the job I do now!

Distinctives

Local campaigning also provides an opportunity to bring two other distinctives as Christians.

Number one, it presents a unique opportunity to listen and learn. Perhaps the best first expression of love and compassion, is listening. It might seem obvious, but it can be quite a radical idea for the church, and one we haven't always been good at putting into practice. Too often we behave as though we don't need to listen because we already have all the answers. But Jesus was a fantastic listener.

On the vast majority of occasions, Jesus healed people because they, or their friends, asked him to. And he directly involved either the person in need or their friends in the healing process. Jesus preserved people's dignity and didn't impose solutions. He asked people what they wanted, then listened, and he often made it clear that it was *their* faith that led to the result. He did not dole out generic blessings to passive recipients – he expected people to participate. When was the last time we asked our neighbours or wider community what they need? There are now great resources, like the Discovery process from Tearfund, to help churches do this. But political engagement almost by definition requires this type of listening, for without it a candidate is fairly sunk.

We should also note that Jesus seems to have been the kind of person that people could go to for help – someone approachable and compassionate, someone who might just listen. You get the sense that people felt he was 'one of us' because he was happy to come to the rough end of town. Are we like that?

Number two – everyone is aware of the sort of negative campaigning that gives politicians a bad name. It is sometimes hard to stand against this tide. However there is a significant impact when people whose hope is not just drawn from what they can see in the visible realm, engage with a community. Our vocabulary can be positive and uplifting rather than cynical and negative. There is optimism, because for the Christian, winning or losing is hopefully not everything. We will fight as hard as anyone, but try never to let a tribal battle trump the interests of the kingdom, sacrificing integrity or relationships. We must never forget where our true identity is found, as it's often all too easy to take refuge in a tribe. The formal coats of political parties and organisations are important to put on, but we must remember that they are only coats.

Final thoughts

Local campaigning creates a natural common ground, which is fertile for relationship-building as Christians. When we work together with people, sharing the highs and lows, lasting bonds are formed. The kingdom extends along the lines created by these pre-existing relationships.

I hope you now have some flavour of what getting politically involved in your locality could look like, and that you can see that it could enhance the mission of your local church, rather than detract from it. My prayer is that we all begin to work for the long-term holistic transformation of our communities as well as embracing the excitement of short-term programmes.

It may still only be a proportion of Christians who will go into politics as candidates, but it should surely be more than we have at present. Perhaps many more could be involved in actively supporting those missionaries for whom their primary mission field is politics – and all of us are called to pray.

There is clearly a strong pragmatic case for the church's involvement in politics. But that should never be enough. The next two chapters build the solid biblical case for engagement that will undergird our adventure.

12

ROUTE 66 – TOURING
THROUGH SCRIPTURE

'When people tell me that the Bible has nothing to do with politics,
I ask them, "Which Bible are you talking about?"'

Desmond Tutu

It is never enough to engage in politics – or anything for that matter – for purely functional reasons. It may limit the mental framework behind our involvement to a simple notion of 'sorting out the world'. Which we can never entirely do, anyway. The call goes much deeper than that. Our role in governance is grounded in our relationship to God. It is a profound vocation and it has echoes all the way back to Genesis and all the way forward to Revelation and beyond. So at this point we stop to look in more detail at what the Bible has to say.

It can be tempting to use Scripture to support and promote an agenda that you are passionate about, but this often means hijacking individual verses as 'poster kids' while happily ignoring others. An argument based on individual verses risks faulty interpretation. A healthier approach is to ask what the whole canon of Scripture has to say about a certain topic. That is obviously a task too large for this book, and so we will point you in the direction of some excellent political theologians at the end of this chapter. However what we will do is go right back to the very start and take a whistle-stop tour through every book of the Bible. It's not hard to find material in every single book that shouts of God's desire for good governance. We could examine each of these in detail, but what is important for now is that you get a sense of how this is not a side issue for God. From beginning to end Scripture makes clear that God is passionate not just about the concept of governance, but the practicalities of how we govern ourselves. Of course this shouldn't surprise us, bearing in mind he invented the whole thing.

We have developed a 'Route 66' tour over the course of the last decade and it seems to be especially well received in our Christians in Politics presentations to theological college students. There is much more that could be said, but hopefully this will whet your appetite to dig a little deeper. Here we go. Take a deep breath . . .

Old Testament

Genesis 1–3

Then God said, 'Let us make mankind in our image, in our likeness, so that they may rule over the fish in the sea and the birds in the sky, over the livestock and all the wild animals, and over all the creatures that move along the ground.'

So God created mankind in his own image,
in the image of God he created them;
male and female he created them.

God blessed them and said to them, 'Be fruitful and increase in number; fill the earth and subdue it. Rule over the fish in the sea and the birds in the sky and over every living creature that moves on the ground.'

Genesis 1:26–28

The LORD God took the man and put him in the Garden of Eden to work it and take care of it.

Genesis 2:15

In short, we are made in his image, so we are called to govern because he governs.

Theologians call this the 'creation mandate' – we are called to faithfully manifest his image in our day-to-day work of stewarding his creation. We rule because we are like our Father. We can take this role seriously or we can do it badly, or we can abdicate our responsibility to others who may lack a biblical worldview. It's worth noting that stewarding creation well goes beyond material things such as plants and animals, to concepts such as freedoms and institutions such as family. There is a cultural mandate to develop institutions for the common good.

These verses in Genesis 1 also make it clear that in this task, our relational priorities are governed by the fact that we are all endowed with equal worth and dignity. In other words, there are no premier league people. Under God's authority, this essential equality is the starting point for all human government.

When we use the phrase 'relational priorities' this refers to the patterns for human-to-human and human-to-God communion laid out in the Bible (and modelled in the Trinity). This can be things like: giving rather than taking; loving rather than hating; accepting the responsibility to be 'my brother's keeper' instead of selfishness; seeking peace; putting others above yourself; stewarding our time and resources for the common good; protecting and promoting the structural and cultural integrity of marriage, parenthood, family life, community and possibly even nation. Understanding the co-dependency between freedom and responsibility – and between justice and mercy. The Sermon on the Mount provides a good overview.

In light of the Fall, politics and government have often been seen as a 'necessary evil' to restrain evil, but this is verging on the functional instrumentalism we mentioned in the introduction. Responsibility for the earth was given to humans even before the Fall. Organisation is still needed in the context of perfection. As we will see from later sections of Scripture, God has always been intending to share his reign with us, and will do so even when evil is no more.

Genesis 37–50   In the story of Joseph we see how God uses his anointed to govern in an alien land for the protection and prosperity of his people and everyone else. Genesis also shows that emancipation from oppression is on God's agenda through the story of the Children of Israel.

Throughout the rest of the Bible, God keeps calling people back to this task of reflecting his image through governance.

Exodus shows Moses was a deeply political figure, again ruling in an alien culture, and we begin to receive the laws that express God's heart for good government. These commandments still form the bedrock of our law. It is important to note that the Children of Israel would not have understood our separation between religious leaders and political leaders. In the Hebrew mindset, God is one, and we are one. Physical, spiritual and mental aspects of our person all combine. In the Exodus itself we see how God cares about all of the person. It does not simply render the Israelites 'spiritually' free. They are also freed economically, politically, and geographically. Their freedom to worship their God is connected to all these other freedoms.

Leviticus has a strong emphasis on personal and corporate morality, and caring for the poor, and shows us how the law is designed to cover all the dimensions of Israel's relations with God, with one another and with the earth. God doesn't just care about the state of our hearts.

Numbers proposes a democratic process under God with the selection of representative leaders.

Deuteronomy affirms the idea of equality under the law for kings and subjects alike. In other words, no one is above the law. This was fleshed out in the UK through the Magna Carta in 1215. Through the Jubilee and Sabbath principles (amongst many others) we see how God cares passionately about how society is ordered.

Joshua shows the need for integrity in leadership, and a strong national identity in which morality is required as a distinctive for God's people.

Judges shows how the Lord raises up and empowers people to lead the nation out of sin, error and judgment. It also shows the need for women to assume national leadership responsibilities.

Ruth shows how social and familial responsibility transcends mere legal contract. Our responsibilities in leadership go beyond the functional letter of the law.

1 and 2 Samuel reaffirm equality under the law for kings and subjects.

1 and 2 Kings charts the good, the bad and the ugly of how to govern. These books show how leaders are subject to greater accountability for their actions.

'Now, LORD my God, you have made your servant king in place of my father David. But I am only a little child and do not know how to carry out my duties. Your servant is here among the people you have chosen, a great people, too numerous to count or number. So give your servant a discerning heart to govern your people and to distinguish between right and wrong. For who is able to govern this great people of yours?'

The LORD was pleased that Solomon had asked for this. So God said to him, 'Since you have asked for this and not for long life or wealth for yourself, nor have asked for the death of your enemies but for discernment in administering justice, I will do what you have asked. I will give you a wise and discerning heart, so that there will never have been anyone like you, nor will there ever be. Moreover, I will give you what you have not asked for – both wealth and honour – so that in your lifetime you will have no equal among kings.

1 Kings 3:7–13

Verse 10 stands out as exposing God's pleasure that Solomon asked for wisdom to govern. It is obviously an issue close to his heart.

1 and 2 Chronicles also show the Lord's heart for government through his reply to Solomon's request for wisdom to govern, and they place the responsibility for national renewal with God's people.

Ezra demonstrates the power of the Word to restore identity and direction to a nation.

Nehemiah teaches about how the restoration of our authority and identity in God brings blessing. It is worth noting here that it is rarely stories of pastors who make it into Scripture. It is the architects, builders, politicians, and kings. God seems to care as much about the practical as the spiritual.

Esther and Mordecai were raised up to lobby the authorities politically to save their people.

Job teaches us about trusting a sovereign God in trials. He is the ultimate authority above any earthly authorities.

> 'Where were you when I laid the earth's foundation?
>   Tell me, if you understand.
> Who marked off its dimensions? Surely you know!
>   Who stretched a measuring line across it?

Job 39:4

The Psalms confirm that God is the ultimate authority, but one who is ready to listen to the cries of his people through praise and petitions. He is a responsive God, caring about the practicalities of victory and defeat, plenty and famine.

Proverbs was written to instruct princes on how to govern when they became kings.

Ecclesiastes talks about the wisdom needed to rule.

Song of Solomon makes clear our relational priorities in light of his authority.

Isaiah describes the coming Saviour and his kingdom – 'of the increase of whose government there shall be no end' (Isaiah 9:7). It paints many vivid pictures of a world whose structures have been utterly restored and redeemed, not left to rot while its inhabitants float off.

> Your ancient ruins shall be rebuilt;
> you shall raise up the foundations of many generations;
> you shall be called the repairer of the breach,
> the restorer of streets to live in.
>
> Isaiah 59:12, NRSV

Jeremiah illustrates the need to speak truth to power. There is also the clear call to

> seek the welfare of the city where I have sent you into exile, and pray to the LORD on its behalf, for in its welfare you will find your welfare.
>
> Jeremiah 29:7, ESV

If ever there was a clear mandate for engagement in all the structures and systems of our locality, here it is.

Lamentations shows how God used one nation to punish another.

Ezekiel describes how the river of true life flowing from the temple is what heals the nations.

Daniel demonstrates that God's people can be called to rule in alien, pagan cultures. There is an implicit recognition that, for engagement in politics, there is a time to defy and a time to comply for the people of God. This was particularly true for Daniel and his three friends. The need for both civic training and a non-negotiable devotional life is apparent. With Daniel we see how integrity is tied to identity, and how the role of the prophetic is important when dealing with governmental power. Importantly, the book also shows that God's dominion covers all kingdoms, all empires and the whole earth – and that, ultimately, all kingdoms will pass into God's own kingdom of love and righteousness.

Hosea attacks hedonism and the abuse of wealth.

Joel promotes truth in the public square.

Amos exposes hypocritical rulers and power elites.

Obadiah affirms that justice cannot be escaped.

Jonah speaks of responsibility beyond the borders of our own race and ethnicity.

Micah emphasises the importance of morality and integrity. Governance must be informed by justice, mercy and humility combined.

Nahum explains how freedom can bring both curses and blessings to a nation.

Habakkuk talks of God's care for the poor.

Zephaniah binds belief to action, and demands clear identity.

Haggai reorders our social priorities in light of God's holiness.

Zechariah reaffirms the absolute authority of God.

... and

Malachi warns against complacency and idolatry in national life.

And that's just the Old Testament! Take another deep breath ...

New Testament

Matthew, Mark, Luke and John The gospels cite the governing supremacy of Christ, particularly through his statement that 'All authority in heaven and on earth is given unto me' (Matthew 28:18); and to Pilate that, 'You would have no power over me unless it had been given you from above' (John 9:11). He confirms God's sovereignty over all secular, unbelieving and pagan governments.

The gospels show that it is important to speak truth to power despite the cost – take, for example, the courage of John the Baptist. In the parable of the sheep and the goats, in Matthew 25:31–46, they show that it is important to speak up for the marginalised and disenfranchised, and that it is vital to proclaim righteousness (the lamp on a stand story, Luke 8:16–18). They show that God gets angry about unrighteousness (Jesus clearing the temple in John 2:13–22); that God hates it when people develop vested interests and oppress and exclude the poor; that wealth can corrupt leaders; that taxes must be set fairly and collected with honesty. They show that peace and reconciliation are priorities (the love your enemies teaching in Matthew 5:43–48); how authority is rightly delegated; why vengeance has no place in justice (an eye for an eye, Matthew 5:38–42). They show that interpreting the times is vital for good decision making; that covenant is more important than contract, both personally and socially; that mercy is vital for impartiality (see what Jesus said about not judging others in Matthew 7:1–5). They show that regard for others cannot be avoided (the commandment to love your neighbour in Matthew 22:39); that leadership must be characterised by faithfulness (in the shepherd and the flock discourse); that mob rule is to be avoided; that manipulating public opinion to subvert justice is wrong; that human rights and civil liberties are important (the false charges against Jesus and his trial for crucifixion are presented as corrupt, for example); why executive transparency and accountability are important; why torture is wrong; why state violence requires restraint by a moral framework; why sacrifice, service and suffering for others is noble; why corruption requires restitution; why forgiveness is essential for governing human relationships. All this can be drawn from the crucifixion story. We see that matter itself will be transformed akin to Jesus' resurrection body in the final resurrection, conveying innate dignity on the 'stuff of now' – the nuts and bolts of the world.

Acts demonstrates a unified and equal community that is governed by council, consensus and majority; illustrates the need to speak truth to power; and proposes new forms of citizenship. It seems that the growth in the early church was to a large extent dependent not only on spiritual virtues but on the fact that no one was in need: a practical, political reality. It also shows the need for religious freedom.

Romans shows the value of secular government; and critiques the human effects of state-sanctioned idolatry. Crucially, in stating that the political authority 'is God's servant for your good'. Paul affirms that political authority comes from God for our benefit, but that our allegiance cannot be unthinking. God is still the ultimate authority:

> Let everyone be subject to the governing authorities, for there is no authority except that which God has established. The authorities that exist have been established by God. Consequently, whoever rebels against the authority is rebelling against what God has instituted, and those who do so will bring judgment on themselves. For rulers hold no terror for those who do right, but for those who do wrong. Do you want to be free from fear of the one in authority? Then do what is right and you will be commended. For the one in authority is God's servant for your good. But if you do wrong, be afraid, for rulers do not bear the sword for no reason. They are God's servants, agents of wrath to bring punishment on the wrongdoer. Therefore, it is necessary to submit to the authorities, not only because of possible punishment but also as a matter of conscience.
>
> This is also why you pay taxes, for the authorities are God's servants, who give their full time to governing. Give to everyone what you owe them: if you owe taxes, pay taxes; if revenue, then revenue; if respect, then respect; if honour, then honour.
>
> Romans 13:1–7

Romans also serves as a reminder of God's concern for all aspects of life on earth, not just the state of hearts. Here innate worth is conveyed to non-human creation in the promise that it will enjoy the same transformation as us:

> I consider that our present sufferings are not worth comparing with the glory that will be revealed in us. The creation waits in eager expectation for the sons of God to be revealed. Or the creation was subjected to frustration, not by its own choice, but by the will of the one who subjected

it, in hope that the creation itself will be liberated from its bondage to decay and brought into the glorious freedom of the children of God.

Romans 8:18–21

1 and 2 Corinthians, in identifying the flawed wisdom of hollow philosophies, establishes the need for moral reference beyond human ideologies; calls believers to model new, subversive forms of community; outlines the ministry of reconciliation; and values suffering for what is right.

Galatians explains the radical, totalising freedom given by Christ and that the gospel both requires and sustains freedom.

Ephesians describes human responsibility in the spiritual battle that informs earthly authority, and states how the church is to communicate 'the manifold wisdom of God ... to the rulers and authorities in the heavenly realms' (Ephesians 3:10). Demonstrating the good governance of the Kingdom is proposed.

Philippians encourages humility and hope in the face of suffering; and challenges abuses related to social status.

Colossians affirms the supremacy of Christ in human affairs by stating that 'Thrones or dominions or authorities – all things were created through him and for him ... and in him all things hold together' (1:16–17). 'All things' here actually means all things – every sphere of human existence, including politics. It also calls for intellectual rigour to challenge hollow philosophies and human traditions.

1 and 2 Thessalonians confirms the value and dignity of labour (with a small 'l'); and asserts the necessity for the rule of law.

---

1 and 2 Timothy compels believers to pray for government 'first of all' – as a priority for the gospel; values the council of elderly people and encourages young people to lead; explains the role of charity; warns against the corruption that wealth can bring; describes a godless society.

> I urge, then, first of all, that petitions, prayers, intercession and thanksgiving be made for all people – for kings and all those in authority, that we may live peaceful and quiet lives in all godliness and holiness. This is good, and pleases God our Saviour, who wants all people to be saved and to come to a knowledge of the truth.
>
> 1 Timothy 2:1–4

These particular verses show that God cares about order, because it reflects the fact that he is a God of order. He brought order from chaos, and continues to do so. Order in human relationships leaves people free to love, free to worship, free to work, and free to explore the depths of God. The gospel often thrives in times of persecution, yes, but rarely in times of anarchy. Order is required for the communication of God's values, which can lead to the building of just structures, which can lead to good governance. Otherwise, salvation is confined to a personal transaction between individuals and God. Personal revival cannot lead to national renewal without order. The freedom to build according to the principles of the kingdom is necessary. Otherwise gains may be fleeting and private.

> Here is a trustworthy saying:
> If we died with him,

> we will also live with him;
> if we endure,
> we will also reign with him.
>
> 2 Timothy 2:11–12

Here our eternal role as priests and kings in the new created order is underlined. These are the roles that we are also called to both exercise and rehearse in the here and now.

Titus discusses authority amongst diverse social groups.

Philemon deals with slavery and labour.

Hebrews confirms the authority structure of heaven, the equality of all people before God, and how justice is indivisible from mercy.

James explains how deeds must accompany words; that favouritism is forbidden in leadership; that a focus upon developing good language and communication is essential for leadership; and how the wisdom that comes from God differs in substance and impact from earthly wisdom.

---

1 Peter calls for believers to 'Be subject for the Lord's sake to every human institution, whether it be to the emperor … or to governors' (2:13 ESV), confirming that all authority is ordained by God, and that submission can be required even during persecution. It also shows that the gospel itself has its place in political power by revealing that Jesus 'has gone into heaven and is at God's right hand – with angels, authorities and powers in submission to him' (3:22).

2 Peter asserts the value of a clear conscience and good teaching for leadership; and the need to respond to evil with good.

1, 2 and 3 John describes the institutional nature of sin; and the need to provide good role models for leadership.

Jude attacks bad role models for leadership; and shows how when abused, authority can be abdicated.

Revelation affirms the dominion of the kingdom of God above earthly empires; calls Christians to lead as well as serve; condemns those who have put their faith in money and power; and promises a conclusion in which justice is inescapable. It shows how redemption in Jesus Christ is not limited to any one area of the creation. Not only persons, but nations, kingdoms, and the entire creation will be reconciled.

> He who was seated on the throne said, 'I am making everything new!'
>
> Revelation 21:5

I hope by now you are convinced that God is concerned not just about the concept of governance, but the nitty-gritty of how it works. He cares not just about the overall strategy but the plan to actually make it happen. You could say that government is the destination and that politics is the car you use to get you there. It is only a vehicle, not an end in itself to be idolised. Sometimes it can be a brash, polluting, inefficient vehicle, but it is better than having no vehicle at all, with the chaos that would ensue.

Huge thanks are due to Dr David Landrum for much of the spine of this chapter and some of the next. I would also point you in the direction of the wonderful book *God and Government* (Theos and SPCK, London 2009) which contains essays from prominent theologians on political engagement. It is essential further reading.

The next chapter is going to summarise some foundations and challenges that spring from our whistle-stop tour through Scripture. As ever, the Bible is a wonderful, yet at times uncomfortable plumb line.

13

FOUNDATIONS FOR
POLITICAL ENGAGEMENT

aving vaulted through Scripture, on what theological assumptions can we base our political engagement? These may seem like unnecessarily theoretical questions, but grim experience has shown that if believers enter into the at times wild world of politics without these firm foundations and the implications that flow from them, they can be quickly blown from their intended course. Sometimes it is dramatic, but more often there is a subtle tapping of the tiller over a period of time until our boat is facing in a very different direction to the one we started in. We'll start with a rather important foundation.

Who is God?

The theologian Chris Wright[1] describes the mission of God in terms of his self-revelation. His primary desire is to make himself known, for he knows that this knowledge and relationship is what humans need to be fully human and thereby whole as individuals, communities or societies. This revelation is about a person, not just about his ways. This is not a purely instrumental mission. So for us, just aiming to end poverty or protect the family cannot be the whole story. Ends cannot justify means with God. How we do something reflects who he is as much as

---

[1] Chris Wright, *The Mission of God: Unlocking the Bible's Grand Narrative* (IVP 2006).

the end product. In politics as much as any other sphere, we can bear no fruit unless we remain in him (John 15:4). We are sadly a generation who often crave instructions rather than intimacy. We want a justified cause, and then want just to get on with it. However we cannot fulfil his mission without reference to him.

But who is he? Again whole books have been written on the subject, so we will not replicate them here. One summary is in Tozer's classic book, *The Knowledge of the Holy* (Authentic 2005). He explains that the God of Scripture reveals himself as wise, infinite, sovereign, holy, three-in-one, omniscient, faithful, loving, omnipotent, self-existing, self-sufficient, just, merciful, eternal, good, gracious and omnipresent. It is quite a list but we need to reflect all of them. The danger is that we emphasise only the aspects of Scripture or God's character that fits with our experience, or that are acceptable to our circle of friends, and in our political engagement we focus exclusively on social justice or exclusively on life issues for example. But his desire for governance is for the totality of his image to be portrayed by his delegated governors, not just a portion of it.

Jesus

Jesus is the perfect 'image of the invisible God' and therefore our primary access point to dig further into his character. And he is an intensely political figure. His message of the kingdom of God directly challenges all earthly powers today in the same way that he challenged the religious leaders of Israel. What we often forget is that when Jesus challenged the religious leaders of his day he was simultaneously challenging Israel's political leaders, as they were one and the same. There was no separation of church and state then. In fact the Jews would not even have understood the question, 'Was Jesus political?' To them he was quite clearly speaking about all of life and throwing down a challenge to all in authority.

Jesus also made it clear that he was the new temple, and this idea is incredibly helpful to our understanding. The temple was not just the spiritual meeting place for the Jews. It was not just a 'church building'. It was also their civic control centre or town hall. As the place where heaven met earth, it was a loud reminder that God cared about every aspect of their lives, not simply their sacrifices of worship. If Jesus is embodying this idea in himself then we can see the obvious implication that his just rule is for every sphere of our lives and of society, not just for inside the four walls of church buildings.

This reality is fleshed out by the following famous incident from his life. One day while he was teaching, a group of Pharisees tried to trap him by asking: 'Is it right to pay taxes to Caesar or not?' (Matthew 22:17, NIV 1984). What they are really saying is: 'Are you a revolutionary, someone opposed to Roman rule; or are you a compromiser, someone who supports Roman rule?' This is a common trap laid for any Christian in politics.

The response of Jesus is devastatingly brilliant. He ignores their flattery, exposes their hypocrisy, and refuses to be tricked into giving a simplistic answer. Jesus reminds us of the way things really are, and what's really important.

He said: 'Give to God what is God's and to Caesar what is Caesar's' (Matthew 22:21, NIV 1984). Jesus reminds us that we should not confuse temporary earthly power with God – the eternal heavenly power. Jesus firmly places all politics, and all government under God's authority.

This passage has been used unhelpfully in the past to drive a wedge between the secular and the sacred, or the political and the spiritual. But here is the crucial mistake. When we talk about what is God's and what is Caesar's we are not talking about two separate realms where God has jurisdiction in the sacred and Caesar has jurisdiction in the secular. It is not like this:

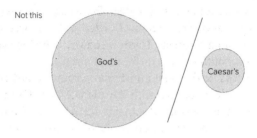

It should actually look more like this:

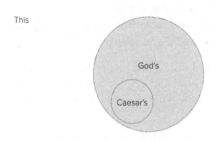

Caesar has a small, delegated area of authority within the context of God's overall authority. God has an opinion on everything including taxes because he is in authority over all of it. Jesus reiterated this when he told Pilate that he would have no authority unless 'it had been given to you from above'. This disallows the old idea that the church should deal with 'spiritual needs' while the government deals with practical needs.

The Franciscan writer Richard Rohr often reminds his readers that there is no such thing as 'secular'.[2] He says that there is only sacred and 'de-sacralised' or desecrated, where humanity has sucked the holiness out of something that was meant for good.

---

[2] See, for example, *Franciscan Mysticism* CD or MP3 download http://www.store.cac.org.

[3] 'God's Grandeur,' in *Poems of Gerard Manley Hopkins*, Robert Bridges (ed) (Humphrey Milford, London 1918).

But nothing can be inherently secular. The Psalmist writes: 'The earth is the Lord's and *everything* in it' (Psalm 24:1). This clearly must include shipping forecasts, Hadron colliders, the life cycles of moths, and party politics.

Or in the words of the poet and hymn writer Gerard Manley Hopkins,[3] 'The world is charged with the glory of God'. He interacts with humanity in an intimate way. In AD 451 the Chalcedon council affirmed the simultaneous divinity and humanity of Christ. We are therefore given a wonderful model for understanding the relationship between the gospel and culture. Jesus' total integration of divine and human leaves us no room for a separation between 'religion' and any other area of our lives.

Former Archbishop of Canterbury Rowan Williams wisely commented on this passage that we must

> 'never forget that the ultimate point of any human political order is giving God what belongs to God – setting human agents free, acknowledging and reinforcing the dignity in which God has clothed them.'[4]

In other words, just as the coin bore Caesar's image, as humans we all bear the image of God, and are therefore to be treated with care and dignity. Managing taxation and the rest of an economic system well is just one way of ensuring this.

One final quote from theologian Jane Collier sums it up,

> 'There is no part of our existence, cultural, political, historical or communal which is not called, through conversion, to become the stuff of which the Kingdom of God is being fashioned.'[5]

Who am I?

In politics, identity is too often easily transferable and contextual. When our identity is up for grabs, so too, sadly, is our integrity and

---

[4] The Most Reverend and Right Honourable Dr Rowan Williams, Archbishop of Canterbury. Sermon given at a Service for the New Parliament: St Margaret's Church, Tuesday, 8 June 2010.

[5] Jane Collier, *From Complicity to Encounter* (Trinity Press International 1998).

purpose. Our rudder will be pushed by the prevailing tide, rather than held by a firm hand on the tiller. As we have mentioned, the identity of present-day political tribes can be just as overpowering as the images of Caesar that commanded worship in the days of the early church. Yet they refused to bow, even when it caused them serious trouble. But lest we think that political identities are the only ones which can usurp our true identity, it is worth noting that those who do not engage in politics may well be accepting identities as consumers rather than participants – ignoring the call to be kings and priests in the new creation. Above all else we need to know who we are in Christ, and who Christ is in us.

Theology, not ideology must be the driver – and our theology (or the mind of Christ) must be formed by the Holy Spirit and the Word of God. In the last century (the 'secular' century) many Christians in public life were either hardened to society, abandoning social engagement to preserve some integrity of faith, or simply compromised – secularised. We need to learn from this.

Who am I? I'm a child of God. I am the righteousness of God in Christ. I'm saved by grace, beloved of God, and I'm on a mission. His mission. Our primary allegiance must be to the King of Kings, and not to any earthly kingdom. That is easy to say, but hard to do in a very tribal political environment. In our fear, we seek the protection of a tribe, so we are tempted to toe the line of the tribe. Let us instead seek the favour and protection of the ultimate authority.

There are some good tests of where our primary allegiances lie. There are our gut responses to statements from those of another political tribe – do we listen for the good in what they say, wanting the kingdom for their lives and their party, or do we have an automatic rejection response to their words and actions. Is there an inner cheering or booing on hearing news of successes and defeats? Do we care more about God's will being done on the earth or our party winning? Do we perhaps believe that those two things are always synonymous?

---

[6] Luther, *Werke* (1900).

Who are we?

Thankfully this particular theological foundation means that we do not have to do this stuff alone. Losing the frame of 'What is *my* mission in life?' and picking up the frame of 'How have *we* been called to participate in *his* mission?' leads to more co-operation, less workaholism and fewer mixed motives.

We are 'the redeemed', the church, and we should live out our identity. Luther called this 'the most controversial doctrine in the Bible'.[6]

But this church is not a building. We are,

> God's household, which is the church of the living God, the pillar and foundation of the truth.
>
> 1 Timothy 3:15

We are those united in Christ and we are a body.

> And he is the head of the body, the church; he is the beginning and the firstborn from among the dead, so that in everything he might have the supremacy.
>
> Colossians 1:18

> I appeal to you, brothers and sisters, in the name of our Lord Jesus Christ, that all of you agree with one another in what you say and that there be no divisions among you but that you be perfectly united in mind and thought ...
>
> 1 Corinthians 1:10

So the more unified we are, the more Christ is embodied and therefore the more blessing ensues. This is a real challenge to Christians who are working in different political parties. We can find unity in our diversity, even while we may disagree on particular aspects of policy and even underpinning ideologies.

> God placed all things under his feet and appointed him to be head over everything for the church, which is his body, the fullness of him who fills everything in every way.
>
> Ephesians 1:22–23

His intent was that now, through the church, the manifold wisdom
of God should be made known to the rulers and authorities in the
heavenly realms.

Ephesians 3:10

So put quite simply, the more salt and light there is in politics,
the more blessing there is for the nation. But we should never
be lone rangers, separated from our brothers and sisters in the
church, because God desires his wisdom to be revealed through
the church – through a community, not an individual.

What is government?

Based on our trip through Scripture, a theological framework for
government looks like this:

- Authority is the exercise of power
- All authority comes from God (you are not in authority,
  unless you are under authority)
- For God, all authority exists for the purpose of government
  (the right ordering or our relational priorities)
- For God all government exists for justice
- For God all justice involves judgment *and* mercy
- God is merciful because he is love
- God judges because he is just
- God is just because he is holy

Again we can see that God's authority is as personal as it is
functional. His holiness is not confined to one area of life. He
craves economic holiness as much as sexual holiness. One is not
more important than the other to him.

On the basis of who God is, who we are, and a biblical view of
government, here are six principles:

1. Government has been instituted by God and should reflect
   God's character, conforming to his design for our relational
   priorities.

2. The role of government is limited and is to restrain evil, judge evil and promote the common good (law is necessarily coercive).

3. Governments can be corrupted by various idolatries.

4. Christians should be model citizens, respect government and engage with it.

5. Christian prayer, service and leadership is important for good government.

6. Christians can never give uncritical allegiance to any state or government, since their first loyalty is to the Lord Jesus Christ.

Some further important points:

Politics is not the same as government. Politics is the method by which human societies struggle to achieve government. Government is the right ordering of our public priorities. In mass societies, this means what we decide to spend money and attention on, and what we don't. The decision to tax this rather than that. To make a treaty with this country rather than that one. Politics is simply the process by which we organise our common life together.

Politics can be idolatrous. It's important because it affects many people in significant ways, but it's not God. The secular compulsion to see a political solution to all things is wrong. Politics is limited.

Interestingly, John Adams, the second President of the USA, said 'Our constitution was made only for a moral and religious people. It is wholly inadequate for the government of any other. Free government rests upon public and private morality. It is not our government that has failed; it is the church that has failed to be the salt of the earth.'[7] What he is suggesting is that a government cannot *produce* morality but can only safeguard those principles which are widely accepted. The authorities can control and punish

---

[7] *The Works of John Adams* (Boston 1854).

lawbreakers and can administrate and bring order to society but only on the basis of widely held ethics. When this ethical foundation changes, the government alone cannot be expected to re-establish it. William Penn, founder of Pennsylvania, said 'Government seems to me to be a part of religion itself. Let man be good and the government cannot be bad.'[8]

Prayer is as important as practice. The Bible calls us to pray for our leaders (1 Timothy 2:1–3) and to remember that our warfare is primarily spiritual (Ephesians 6:11–13).

We won't go too far wrong if we pray familiar prayers like this one:

> *The Third Collect for Grace from the Book of Common Prayer. (Morning Prayer)*
>
> O Lord our heavenly father, Almighty and Everlasting God, who has safely brought us to the beginning of this day; Defend us in the same with thy mighty power, and grant that this day we fall into no sin, neither run into any kind of danger; but that all our doings may be ordered by **thy governance** to do always what is righteous in thy sight; through Jesus Christ our Lord. AMEN[9]

Religion and politics

However we should not be surprised to find that the chemical reaction of religion and politics can be fraught with danger. How can we expect it to be any other way, when being part of that intentional combustion follows directly in the footsteps of one who was crucified for doing the same. It is a risky business. It is a risky business because authority is contested ground. The principalities and powers (and sadly sometimes we, the church) are keen to keep religion and politics separate because life is a lot less messy that way. Keeping them comfortably separate suits many agendas. Time and time again people of faith are not engaged

---

8 Frame of Government of Pennsylvania, 1682.
9 *The Book of Common Prayer* (OUP, Oxford 1662).

with but told to get back in their box. I have been present twice at Downing Street receptions where two separate Prime Ministers have unintentionally given away their belief in a secular/sacred divide. Listeners were told not to worry because legislation would not 'affect what happens in your churches'. It was as if the church was being told the only thing it needed to worry about was what happened within its four walls. Having opinions on how the rest of society is ordered was simply not our job. Truly painful. We need to challenge that nonsense, but we also need to be wise to the context and realise that we may make much more headway if we speak more as the church dispersed rather than the church gathered. We may be much more effective as the politician or journalist than as the official spokesperson of the church fighting for space in the public square.

What is the lie of the land?

There isn't time here to go into the strong Christian influences within the three historic political parties without a total lack of nuance. I will instead point you in the direction of three fantastic publications from the Partisan Project by the Bible Society. The extent of the early Christian influences in each of the parties is startling and also sobering, providing a challenge to those who would follow in those footsteps to restore some of that initial charism.

Paul Bickley, *Building Jerusalem? Christianity and the Labour Party* (Bible Society 2010)

TASTER: The Labour party was formed by a fusion of Unions and Christian Socialists in the early 1900s. Did you know that one-quarter of Labour MPs in the 1920s were Methodist lay preachers? Keir Hardie, F. D. Maurice, and R. H. Tawney are all revered party figures who were also believers.

Stephen Backhouse, *Experiments in Living: Christianity and the Liberal Democrat Party* (Bible Society 2010)

TASTER: In the late 1800s under the leadership of William Gladstone (an evangelical Christian) the Liberal Party was largely made up of nonconformists and was particularly prominent in Wales which had recently experienced a revival amongst its churches. These threads were hugely influential in seeding our present-day concepts of freedom and equality.

Joshua Hordern, *One Nation but Two Cities: Christianity and the Conservative Party* (Bible Society 2010)

TASTER: It is without doubt that William Wilberforce has been one of the most influential figures in the Conservative Party's history. Edmund Burke, Adam Smith, and Benjamin Disraeli are other figures whose thinking has been influential, all of whom drew strongly from their faith.

These books and similar information about other political parties are all available from www.christiansinpolitics.org.uk

Honest critique

If you think you can find plenty of reasons to be disapproving of politics and politicians, believe me, I can find more. I live there. I am not blind to all of the following and more ...

- Pragmatic managerialism – policies and practice that have no moral roots.
- Vacuous rhetoric – where 'values' are often quoted but rarely defined.
- Political production line clones who have never had real jobs, or have never been part of wider civic society organisations like clubs, unions, churches or guilds – thereby having a lack of connection with ordinary people.
- Ugly tribalism – parties spending more on attacking one another than on policy research.

I could go on, but you get the picture. I see all of these things as reasons to get more deeply involved, not to run in the opposite direction. What if Jesus had so despaired with the state of the planet that instead of coming to earth, he stayed comfortable in his heavenly dwelling? To follow Christ is to be honest about the huge dysfunction and then choose to do something about it, even if that costs us. For him, it not only cost him his life, but his respectability, and status. Are we prepared also to make those sacrifices?

I see much that is difficult and flawed in politics, but here are some of the other things I see:

- I see people who give up many of their evenings and weekends to knock on doors in their neighbourhoods, or sometimes at the other end of the country.

- I see people who are affected by the situations of need that they come across, and who then try to formulate policies that will help.

- I see people who are willing to do the hard yards of writing policy proposals – assimilating statistics and research, consulting experts, and starting pilot studies. They do this in the knowledge that their proposals will be critiqued and mocked by a wide variety of people. This is a far cry from just 'sharing your thoughts' on a blog.

- I see people who could often be making more money in other lines of work.

- I see people who are deeply affected by the vicious personal criticism that often comes their way.

- I see people who cope with the blows of arguments and power struggles, but pick themselves up and keep on going.

- I see people who have invested large amounts of time in working out how to make government work. It is not easy or pretty work. The bureaucracy is huge.

- I see people who are unselfish in their desire to support one another.

- I see people who listen with grace to the stories of those who are very different to them, and I see them grow in the process.
- I see people who desperately want this country to be a better place to live.
- Above all, I see people who are actually remarkably like me, but often more patient, more passionate, and more committed. I learn a lot.

What are some of the advantages of engaging in politics?

We have spoken about the benefits to society of Christians getting involved in party politics in terms of being 'salt and light'. What we have not highlighted are the personal benefits of getting involved.

- The privilege of frequently meeting members of the public and hearing their joys and struggles.
- The sense of mission and camaraderie that comes from a shared task – especially when that shared task is trying to make life better for all the citizens of the country.
- The stretching of faith and dependence on prayer.
- The need to clarify and hone what you believe in the face of opposition.
- The opportunities to bless people in simple ways – sorting out blocked gutters, dangerous dogs, or planning permission problems.
- The 'bird's eye view' of what is going on in our country.
- The wisdom you accrue from working with those who have been learning to govern for some time.
- The hope that you are reflecting your Maker's image in a profound way, by exercising your vocation to lead.

What are some of the societal dangers of engaging in politics?

Christendomism

Whether we are talking about the days of Constantine or strands of present-day neo-conservative imperialism, Christendomism represents an inability to let go of the need to control through centralised authority. We believe in God and we force him on everyone else. There is an inability to accept plurality as a reality in which human agency and choice is God-given. It is unbiblical and historically totally disastrous. It reflects a secularisation of church, driven by church seeing culture as irredeemable.

Progressivism

Here we could reference aspects of the social gospel movement and liberalism. We are trying to build the kingdom on earth by ourselves. Again this is unbiblical and historically totally disastrous. It reflects a secularisation of church, driven by church seeing culture as Christ.

Distinct from the practicalities of improvement or sustained benefits in raised living standards, the political application of the philosophy of human progress is what gives us progressivism. Progressives propose that today is better than yesterday, just because it's today. At its heart is a dangerous delusion: the idea that, despite what every history book in every library on earth tells us, human nature is essentially good, getting better and even perfectible.

If we cannot agree on a fixed point to which we are progressing, the only option left to provide a sense of momentum forward is to move away from other fixed points. If there is no shared vision of what we are moving towards then our only option is to move away from shared moral roots. Hence the drive to free ourselves from various previously assumed roots about family and duty.

This headlong rush towards an imagined better future without the person of the Creator being involved leads to another dangerous conclusion. Namely, that the means are now justified by the ends. Everything including life itself becomes instrumental, and all without a blueprint or parameters. Without someone who cares how things are done as well as what is done, we become mere economic units. If we can be arranged in a way that represents progress then whether we are trampled or not along the way does not matter.

A corporate culture like that of the failed energy giant Enron fleshed out this survival of the fittest. A Dawkinsesque evolutionary philosophy pervaded their culture, with its inevitable consequences.

An inconvenient, yet rather obvious truth about progress lacking a compass, points towards the deeper, religious roots of the idea of progress. Being all about studying the highest end for humanity and then working to bring this about, it is not hard to discern the biblical contours of the ideal. Indeed, widely regarded as a copy of the teleology of the doctrine of the Kingdom of God, John Gray has called progressivism a 'shoddy replica of Christian faith markedly more irrational than the original article, and in recent years more harmful'.[10]

The present political orthodoxy of progressivism was writ large at a party conference fringe debate a few years ago. A questioner from the floor asked a question about abortion, and the MP on the panel replied, 'I think that is a twentieth century issue, not a twenty-first century issue. The discussion has moved on.'

Incredible

Without actually entering into the debate on the rights and wrongs of a policy, it is brilliantly written off simply because it is of yesterday, and by the tenets of progressivism, what is of today must inevitably be better than what is of yesterday. Watch out for the regular use of this language on TV and radio debates. Another manifestation is the phrase, 'We need to be on the right side of history.' In this case, hilariously, time itself is providing the moral plumb line, which (it does not take a rocket scientist to work out),

---

[10] John Gray (2004: 41).

it is singularly ill-equipped to do. Also note that only time which is marching forward is allowed to provide the plumb line. Rarely now do we make the argument that time in reverse would have anything to offer, or in fact that there is wisdom from elders and history to be gleaned.

These forces which form the wider cultural milieu help to explain the limitations of politics and the importance of believers infiltrating the worlds of education, the arts, the media and academia. Politics is far from all-important. But it is important, and the next chapter helps to explain why it makes a practical difference to the lives of many people, joining the dots between legislation and normal life.

Recommended reading

Tim Keller, *Generous Justice: How God's grace makes us just* (Hodder & Stoughton 2010)

David T. Koyzis, *Political Visions and Illusions: A survey and Christian critique of contemporary ideologies* (InterVarsity Press, USA 2003)

Craig G. Bartholomew and Michael W. Goheen, *Living at the Crossroads: An introduction to Christian worldview* (Baker 2008)

Nick Spencer and Jonathan Chaplin, *God & Government* (SPCK 2009)

John Gray, *Black Mass: Apocalyptic religion and the death of utopia* (Penguin 2007)

Jonathan Haidt, *The Righteous Mind: Why good people are divided by politics and religion* (Penguin 2012)

14

JOINING THE DOTS

Sometimes we don't see how politics is relevant to the many issues that we care about as Christians. There are times when we find it much easier to be publically vocal about poverty, marriage or war than actually part of framing legislation that has a profound impact on those areas. Do we care more about being on the right side of the argument than actually effecting change?

I have already mentioned how Christian campaigners worked together with other groups of Christians working on the inside of politics to effect change in the area of aid restrictions and the World Bank. Here we look at two more issues to illustrate how politics is essential for joining the dots.

Trafficking

In the last decade Christians have become increasingly passionate about the issue of people trafficking. The horrendous statistics and stories have roused us into action. We have delivered petitions, taken part in vigils, walked through towns dressed as bar codes, and sent millions of emails. We have also set up organisations to take direct action and worked with police to expose those who control this terrible trade. We have lobbied local authorities to crack down on known establishments. Organisations such as International Justice Mission (IJM), Hope for Justice, Stop the Traffik and the Salvation Army – along with former Conservative MP Anthony Steen – have been tirelessly working to combat the crime of slavery on our doorstep. What may be less obvious is the role of those

Christians who have been working behind the scenes. They will not be standing on platforms, issuing rallying cries or press releases, but their work is no less vital. All the passion in the world is of little use unless our laws allow the police and other agencies to take effective action to prosecute or protect. It is in this regard that members of the Conservative Christian Fellowship (CCF) have been instrumental in channelling this energy and translating it into meaningful legislation.

Members of the CCF were able to bring these campaigning organisations into Parliament to meet with backbenchers, Ministers and Secretaries of State. This, along with the combined efforts of Christians on the Left and the Liberal Democrat Christian Forum as well as research from the Centre for Social Justice, has allowed the draft Modern Slavery Bill to gain support across the House and make tackling this issue a reality. Any legislation requires an enormous amount of work to ascertain whether it will actually achieve what it is designed to achieve. The devil is often in the detail. The only way of making sure is to talk to the experts in the field, and, as the details of civil prevention orders for traffickers and victim protection strategies were mooted, the wisdom of these Christian organisations was vital in spotting loopholes for traffickers, or highlighting the current gaps in resource for victims. The strength of relationships that had been developed between Christian MPs, Christian organisations with expertise and government ministers meant that these discussions were honest and fluent. Those involved in the draft Bill have been clear that they improved and accelerated the process. These sorts of relationships were only possible through the day-to-day ongoing work of the CCF. We all know that we prefer to work with and take advice from those that we trust. Without building this trust with politicians within the parties, all our convictions may cause little impact, no matter how passionate they are.

Though there is some discussion and disagreement amongst all of the parties on the detail and application of this draft Bill, it cannot be denied that it would not have achieved the priority and prominence it has were it not for the lobbying of believers, but also the vital role of those believers who are quietly joining the dots.

It is the first Bill of its kind in Europe, and therefore will, when it gains Royal Assent, bear echoes of the achievements I mentioned in the introduction of the great reformer William Wilberforce who, compelled by his Christian conviction, engaged in politics to end the slave trade. It's clear that Christians still have an important role to play in setting the standard, providing vision and realising justice for the most vulnerable in society.

Sunday Trading

You may remember that in 2012, not long before the Olympics, the Government proposed a Bill temporarily suspending Sunday trading laws for the duration of the Games. The legislation was to be enacted for the whole country, not just areas where Olympic events were taking place. Instead of only opening for six hours on a Sunday, larger shops would be able to open all day.

Large retailers had wielded considerable influence in parliament to give the idea some legs. The bill was tabled rapidly in an attempt to rush the legislation through, taking many by surprise. Party leaderships were loath to oppose it in case they should be portrayed as 'anti-Olympics' (A fate worse than death, apparently. I was a big fan of the Olympics!). Behind the scenes the word from the Labour party hierarchy was that Labour MPs would be encouraged to vote with the Government because this was a temporary measure. In fact it was to be a three-line whip, that is, a strong encouragement to vote with the party line, and potential consequences if you don't.

Those who had been working on this sort of legislation before were convinced that it was a thinly disguised attempt by the large retailers to lay the ground for future wholesale liberalisation of Sunday trading laws. They would be able to say, 'Look how well it worked during the Olympics,' 'No lives were lost,' 'Look how much money we brought in.' This was of course flatly denied by those pushing the legislation. As Christians on the Left, we refused this utilitarian view of life, where money rules everything. We believe in protecting family life, and sustainable working arrangements. Individuals, families, communities and the whole of society benefits from having a fallow day to take stock, worship and rest. Of course life is more complicated than that for most, but we should surely protect any specialness that we do have left, before we slide further into an Americanised non-stop consumption model.

We held a meeting of the Christians on the Left parliamentary group. During this meeting our chair, Alun Michael MP, pointed out that there was precedent for this issue being a free vote of conscience. When Tony Blair asked him to deal with this brief he had said, 'Yes, but I don't think you are going to like what I think about it!' Tony therefore didn't give him the brief but was content for him to articulate his alternative view. One of our members was Susan Elan Jones MP who worked in the whips' office. She was then able to go back to her team and register the temperature of our MPs on the subject. By the time we reached Friday, a three-line whip had become a one-line whip, and over the weekend it became a free vote, meaning MPs could vote as they wished.

That meant we had fuller freedom to hit the phones on the Monday and rally support for voting 'No'. We emailed every MP with a comprehensive briefing paper explaining the arguments put together by ourselves and the Keep Sunday Special campaign. Working alongside some unions, in the next 48 hours we managed to convince 153 MPs to vote against the Bill.

Sadly the vote was still carried, but we made enough noise to cause the powers that be to think again before attempting another extension. So far it hasn't happened. Having said that, as we predicted, almost as soon as the Olympic Games were over, some of the usual suspects popped up to say, 'Well, it's worked so well, why don't we extend it ...'

In retrospect, it was another example of what Christians can achieve when we find common cause with folks from other agencies and other parties. All the passion in the world from church members sending emails or postcards means little unless it can be translated into this kind of work on the inside.

These examples show a little more about how being involved in a political party means you can be part of the upstream team, working to change unjust structures or establish better structures to protect the most vulnerable.

The hub of so many crucial decisions like these, as we have seen, is our Parliament at Westminster. In the next chapter we are going to take a look inside those hallowed walls to discover some things you may not have seen on your TV screens.

15

WESTMINSTER

It is a privilege to walk around the halls of Westminster. The incredible history is carved into sculptures, painted in murals and etched in stone for all to see. I love the stories that those who come on parliamentary tours are told about tennis balls from the seventeenth century being found in the roof of Westminster Hall, or suffragettes chaining themselves to statues. But there are some things that the official tour won't tell you. You cannot get away from the fact that God is 'in the walls'. That's whether we are talking about the Judaeo-Christian principles on which our very democracy is based, or the huge influence Scripture and the church have on the fabric of the building itself.

There are the angels looking down on parliamentarians from every angle in many parts of the Palace. They remind anyone passing below where the real authority lies. There is the huge, dramatic painting of a very early piece of legislation which hangs at the top of Westminster Hall. It depicts Moses receiving the stone tablets on which the Ten Commandments were written. How I wish more parliamentarians would glance up at it as they leave the building.

If you move on up through St Stephen's Hall you come to a striking painting of a crowd of medieval-looking folks crowded around a book. On closer inspection, you will read this inscription: 'In spite of persecution, Christians meet in secret to read Wycliffe's version of the Bible'. I often think that the guy in the canary yellow hat wasn't too worried about being discovered, but it's still another striking statement about how Scripture is present in the foundations of our nation and its Parliament.

Even if you have never been inside Parliament, you may well have heard the chimes of Big Ben, either on TV or walking around London. The tuneful chime that happens every fifteen minutes is very difficult to describe in words – it starts ding-dong-ding-dummm. It is called the 'Westminster Quarters'. I would recommend finding it on Youtube. It is based on a section of Handel's Messiah and interestingly what it is ringing out to the Palace of Westminster and much of the surrounding area, nay, the world, are these words:

> *All through this hour*
> *Lord, be my guide*
> *And by Thy power*
> *No foot shall slide.*

It is a tangible reminder for those with ears to hear, that there is a higher authority at work, whose wisdom is open and available if only we would seek it.

If I am bringing people into the Houses of Parliament I always stop with them for a few minutes to get them to pray with me in the middle of the Central Lobby. At that point you can look one way and see the throne from which the Queen delivers her speech in the House of Lords, and look the other way and see the famous green leather of the Speaker's chair in the House of Commons. It is quite a spot.

If you look upwards there are the huge mosaics in all four directions depicting St George, St Patrick, St David and St Andrew. I am unashamedly proud of my own patron saint, Patrick, and love the fact that his grassroots movement of whole life mission is honoured in this splendid place. It serves as a potent reminder to those who may believe that all power is exercised from the top down. But best of all, if you look downwards you can see some Latin words inscribed in the border of the rose-piece tile arrangement on the floor. Thousands of people walk across this central point of parliament every day. It sits directly between the two Houses, and represents the epicentre of democracy in the 'mother of all parliaments' which has been the model for many others around the world. But few know what the Latin they trample over actually says. It is Psalm 127:1: 'Unless the Lord builds the house, the workers labour in vain.' There, right in the foundations, at the very core of the building you might say, is a profound and prophetic statement. And boy, do we need to hear it. Sadly, there is plenty of 'vain labour' in those corridors and halls. But how fantastic that those words have echoed through the centuries into the ether, calling those who lead also to serve and calling those who lead also to listen.

While we are talking about that public lobby, the central area you often see TV news reporters broadcasting from, it is worth stopping to realise something. That space is where the word 'lobbying' comes from: the concept of making your case to your Member of Parliament started there. And in fact it still takes place there. It is a public lobby in a public building. The airport-style security checks sadly convince people that Parliament is not an open access public building. But it is. You can still walk up to the desk in the public lobby and ask to see your MP. This is called 'green-carding'. They will appear within 45 minutes or their staff will give the reason why they can't – a parliamentary fact-finding trip to Uzbekistan for example. Obviously I wouldn't recommend this as the most reliable method of connecting with your MP, but you never know! The public lobby was where 'ordinary' members of the public milled around rubbing shoulders with parliamentary 'members' sharing their concerns, and bringing important intelligence as to what was happening out in the country.

The assumption that you need an appointment, or that you cannot just enter Parliament as a citizen is part of the false wall we are trying to break down with this book. There is no sharp dividing line between politicians and everyone else. There is no elevated intellectual or spiritual plane on which they operate. The interface between people and politics should be porous. I hear stories all the time of MPs who have taken up certain causes purely because they received a phone call or a letter from a constituent. They take that part of their job extremely seriously.

Let's take the short walk from central lobby down into the commons chamber. The first thing that strikes you is how much smaller it is than it appears on TV. You struggle to imagine how 650 MPs could fit into this small space – and in fact, they don't! You notice the perspex screen erected in front of the public gallery just months before a spectator turned participant in 2004. In what you can only describe as an excellent shot, Ron Davies (not the ex-MP) hurled a condom full of purple paint and hit Tony Blair on his right shoulder. I was watching it live, as I waited for my niece Hannah to be born. What I didn't know at the time was this: the Prime Minister at that moment was standing at one of the two 'despatch boxes'. It is across these boxes that the Prime Minister and Leader of the Opposition cross swords at Prime Minister's Questions. What most folks don't know is that these gold-encrusted props are actually real boxes, and that the boxes contain Bibles. They were the gift of the good people of New Zealand quite some time ago. Hands are placed on them before speaking for the same reason that, in a courtroom, an oath is taken by placing one's hand on a Bible. When a minister makes a statement to the House of Commons, they are in effect giving testimony. I find it powerful to think those ancient manuscripts still sit inside those boxes, whispering eternal truths to anyone that will listen amidst the noise.

Westminster Hall

I first walked into Westminster Hall eleven years ago. It is a huge space, a palace built in the eleventh century, which is the reason we still call it 'the palace of Westminster'. It was the last Anglo-Saxon King's palace, and eventually Henry VIII gifted it to the people so they could discuss the affairs of the nation. (Before we admire the largesse, it should be noted however that 'the people' in question were not exactly commoners!)

You would recognise it in recent times as the place where the Queen Mother was laid in state in 2002 as thousands queued to pay their respects, or where Nelson Mandela and Barack Obama addressed both Houses of Parliament.

In Westminster Hall you are literally walking all over history. On the floor lie plaques to the Queen's father, her grandfather, Winston Churchill, and many more who lay in state there. There are also reminders of moments of crisis with a plaque commemorating the very spot where Thomas More was sentenced to death in 1535.

On that first day I walked in, my breath was taken away by the scale and the beauty of the place. But I also felt a nudge from God. He said the most ridiculous thing. It went something like this: 'One day you will lead hundreds of people in worship from those steps.' At the top of the hall are the grand steps which form a kind of stage for various State occasions. I laughed at the thought, presuming that my megalomania was getting the better of me, putting words in God's mouth. As it was the first time I had ever set foot in the place, obviously the majesty of the space was doing something to my brain. I also thought it was a ridiculous idea, as someone had told me that there were by-laws dating back centuries prohibiting live music in the Palace in an attempt to suppress mischief-making! But those words stayed with me.

Over the course of the next couple of years I would attend the weekly parliamentary prayer gathering as often as I could, gradually getting to know various believers who worked in Parliament. The place had a strange pull. I was never sure whether it was the classic pull of power and prestige or whether God really was saying something. I would often sit praying in Parliament Square, staring up at Big Ben.

I was then asked to help with the worship for the lunchtime service. This involved smuggling my guitar through the X-ray machines. To understand how entertaining that is, you need to know that inside my guitar there are a lot of wires attached to the wood via blobs of blu-tak like putty. It could not look more like a bomb if it tried! But there seemed to be favour with the powers that be, and we were allowed to make some noise. To be honest, I then forgot about the word I felt I'd had from God, for a few years. Then the National Prayer Breakfast, which had previously taken place in the Queen Elizabeth Conference Centre, was moved into Westminster

Hall. A couple of years later I was asked to lead worship for the event. Previously the music had been quite traditional. However the prayer breakfast always had a stage at the side of the hall near different ornate steps towards some meeting rooms, not at the far end where I had stood and apparently heard God. I laughed to myself as I thought, 'God you nearly got it right, but close enough'. But just leading worship in that space was good enough for me. Then I walked in at 5:30am on the morning of the prayer breakfast and the organisers had rotated the seating 90 degrees. The stage and mics were set up at the far end! I couldn't believe it. God has a sense of humour. It was an amazing experience and privilege to stand there and see hundreds of hands raised in that place that has such history. It was as if we were joining in song with thousands of forefathers and the overlooking angels. The stones really did cry out. Interestingly, since that year the stage has always been back facing the traditional way again!

The history of the London Parliament underlines a crucially important fact, which is often overlooked in present-day discussions about faith in the public square. The concept of a plural public square was the gift of the church to the world. It was Augustine who first spoke of the *saeculum*, from which we derive the word secular. It was never designed to be a separate territory from the sacred, but an open space that anyone was free to inhabit whatever religion they practised, or if they practised none at all. In the years to come, it may be the death of pluralism we should mourn as much as Christian public influence.

The creep of *totalitolerance* is unnerving. Examples of an increasing inability to accept that people will have views different or opposed to the assumed norms of popular culture are plentiful. Views being discounted purely because they were given by a Christian expert during the reading of the HFE (Human Fertilisation and Embryology) Bill in the 2005–10 Parliament was a particular low point. This is why we should not allow the encouraging news of 'God in the walls' of parliament to soothe us into lethargy or apathy. It should serve as a reminder that good roots produce good fruit and bad roots produce bad fruit. Our decisions and culture leave a legacy to those who follow along behind us. What would be assumptions for us may not be for them.

Sometimes things need to be crystallised as reminders of not just our values, but more importantly where those values come from. The word 'values' gets used a lot in the public square. Everyone wants their policies to have the feel of something profound, so often values are retrofitted to policies to give them some gravitas. But the concept of values is a tricky one which is hard to pin down. For example, my sense of what 'equality' means can lead me in a very different directions to someone else. Values can easily be free-floating and serve a functional purpose, rather than be the non-negotiable anchors that we hope for. People used to talk about morals, and you could trace them to their roots. In our own fallenness and humility we shy away from talking about morals, for fear of being 'moralising' but I wonder whether that fear has gone too far. We live in an age crying out for fixed points of reference. If people do not find them in God, they will find their fixed points in nationalism, or economic survivalism, and we are sadly seeing more and more of this already.

But what of the present day in parliament?

Underneath Westminster Hall is the beautiful chapel of St. Mary Undercroft, which has now been restored to its former glory after Oliver Cromwell turned it into stables for his horses. You could not have a better example of the fight between functionality and beauty – there is now a lot of gold leaf down there.

It has been my privilege for the last few years to lead the monthly worship gatherings that happen in the chapel of St. Mary. At these meetings politicians of all parties come together alongside other staff from around the Palace of Westminster. There are researchers, librarians, security staff and catering workers. There have been many times when we have shared together in prayer while matters of huge importance are being discussed not far above us. We are often praying 'Your will be done, your kingdom come' without knowing exactly what that will looks like in a given debate, but nonetheless it feels important to offer up our prayers. There are also weekly communion services, masses, Bible studies, and Alpha groups. Many groups from outside of Parliament also come in to hold prayer gatherings on a regular basis. Most exciting of all however are the groups of MPs and peers from different parties who meet together in private to share fellowship across the great divides. The extent to which this happens is one of the great, untold stories of Parliament. If all you see of Parliament is Prime Ministers' Questions, it is hard to understand how this is possible, but it is. Not only do these MPs and peers meet to pray with one another, they actually share life. Their families are connected. The friendships are deep.

There have been many occasions where the strength of these relationships has meant cross-party problems were headed off before they became too large to control. This has led to others engaging in similar relationship-building, rather than falling into the usual pattern of sticking mostly to their own tribe. It is one of the most profound gifts that Christians can bring to Parliament. They can bring a spirit of reconciliation that seeks to find common ground rather than potentiate the divisions. Or when the honest disagreements remain, there is a spirit that seeks to 'play the ball and not the (wo)man'. There are ways you can make an argument which do not cast aspersions on the character of those on the other side of the argument. It is sadly often the faster route to simply throw mud, but the principled parliamentarian stands out in their desire to treat everyone with civility. This is much easier to do when you are coming from a theological position that acknowledges we are all fallen and that we all see through a glass darkly and only see in part.

An interesting development in Parliament in the last fifteen years has been the new building – Portcullis House. It houses the offices of a large number of MPs and has a huge glass-covered atrium where people meet for food and drink. This atrium has in many ways become the epicentre of a lot of parliamentary business. The chances of just bumping into people are greatly increased. Rather than the hidden bars and cafes of the rest of the parliamentary estate, which easily become the haunts of one tribe or the other, here everyone is visible in broad daylight. 'Opponents' continually rub shoulders and make eye contact as they walk back and forth. I believe it has had a powerful humanising effect on the place. It is a great place to sit and pray for all those who are seated or walking through. Many a chance conversation has proved significant for the kingdom. It has certainly helped to make Parliament more 'porous' – allowing easy meetings between members of the public and parliamentary staff.

In case you are still in any doubt about the 'God in the walls' factor at Westminster, have a read at the first words spoken on any day where there is parliamentary business in the House of Commons.

> 'Lord, the God of righteousness and truth, grant to our Queen and her government, to Members of Parliament and all in positions of responsibility, the guidance of your Spirit. May they never lead the nation wrongly through love of power, desire to please, or unworthy ideals but laying aside all private interests and prejudices keep in mind their responsibility to seek to improve the condition of all mankind; so may your kingdom come and your name be hallowed. Amen.'[1]

What a wonderful, realistic and streetwise prayer! The Speaker's chaplain, Rev Rose Hudson-Wilkins, always reports with pleasure that MPs whom she never expects, who are 'officially' unbelieving, often sneak into the chamber in time for the prayers.

As the previous Speaker's Chaplain, Canon Robert Wright says,

> The Prayers for Parliament are an important pointer and reminder and challenge. They point to God's reign over all things, they remind us that God is committed to and involved in his world and they challenge us not to get caught up in our own little worlds but to be open to God's possibilities in all things.[2]

---

[1] Parliamentary Prayers.
[2] Canon Robert Wright, 'God in governance' (Industrial Christian Fellowship Lecture, 2004).

In summary, I hope you can see that Parliament is a place where you could feel at home (in one sense) as a believer, rather than feeling like an outsider. The same applies to the Scottish Parliament at Holyrood and to the Assemblies in Cardiff and Belfast. The same applies to your local council chamber. Women and men have been forerunners for the kingdom in these places. They would be the first to say that they have made their fair share of mistakes, but they have also ploughed a furrow, which makes it easier for others to follow. There is no need to fear. Many Members of Parliament mention to me how they genuinely sense the support of peoples' prayers. This is not a job you will be doing on your own.

16

SO HOW ARE WE GOING
TO DO THIS?

I am not a fan of books that lay out a dramatic problem, yet fail to provide potential solutions. I am not a fan of books that lay out a vision of how things could be different, but fail to provide tangible baby-steps to get there. There is a real danger of this in a book about politics especially. The end points can seem so abstract or far removed from our reality that we sit back in resigned frustration. Fifteen years ago, the idea of being involved in politics was mere fantasy to me, but it is now a very present reality. You have seen how that happened gradually for me and for many other believers in this book. My hope is that our stories encourage you that it is possible, but they are not intended to provide definitive blueprints for how you do it. God will weave his purposes through many different types of journey. Having said that, there are some helpful foundational steps that can help you in the right direction (or the left direction!). In this chapter we will explore some of those, so you are not left informed and inspired, but disempowered.

As we have already mentioned, the gospel grinds up against every subculture in different ways. In any given country or job there are endemic strongholds which need challenging. In the financial industry it may be selfishness and greed, in the media it may be obsession with the shallow and immediate. In the church it is .... (insert your suggestion here!). In politics it is often an economy with the truth, tribalism, workaholism and self-promotion. Interestingly, the most common complaint I hear from many politicians is how lonely it is. Not too many people really understand the pressures you are under. These pressures lead politicians to indulge in the escapism and excess that has all too often made tabloid headlines. There is trail of broken marriages and relationships all over Westminster.

That's why, as the Christian groups within the parties train our future candidates, we are encouraging them, 'Yes, we are going to do this,' but we are also saying, 'But we are going to do it differently.' Which may well mean doing it more slowly. We are not aiming for the fast burn method so beloved of the newspapers, where people go from zero to hero to zero again in the space of a few years. That would get us more air time, but that's not what we are after.

In late 2013, as I was praying and preparing what I might say at the parliamentary re-launch of 'Christians on the Left', the phrase, 'They came expecting fireworks' dropped into my mind. It seemed an appropriate starting point for an event happening in the Houses of Parliament on the night of the 5th of November!

It's in the nature of a launch, with a new website (which had already been visited by people from 42 different countries), a storm of Twitter messages and huge amounts of enthusiasm in the room (140 people squeezed into every crevice of Committee Room 11), to expect some fireworks and glitz. I was able to encourage everyone that in the 24 hours since the site had gone live we had already accrued a raft of new members. Energy was high.

So when I stood up to speak I said this ...

In first century Palestine, they also came looking for fireworks. An oppressed people were looking for liberation and they wanted it now. They were hoping for a mighty explosion of energy and light that would restore their status as God's chosen people, back in charge of their own destiny. They were looking for a military extravaganza. And it seemed that this carpenter from Nazareth was going to light the touchpaper.

The thing is, they came looking for fireworks, but instead they got a man telling stories about something practically invisible. What they got was one who said 'The Kingdom of heaven is like a mustard seed.' He meant, 'This isn't going to be fast. This is going to be slow.' He also meant, 'This isn't going to start big, it's going to start infinitesimally small.' The Japanese theologian Kosuke Koyama wrote a book about this kingdom called *Three mile an hour God* (SCM 1979). Our God seems to move slowly, because he moves at the speed of relationships. For him ends never justify means. For him it is about people, and he cares as much about the journey as the destination. He cares as much about the method as the product delivered. That is why it is a long, slow journey. That is why in politics especially, we must be in it for the long haul. We are in it for the long haul because we care about people. We care about process as well as product.

We must not get sucked into the instant culture of the twenty-first century, where everything is about overnight sensations and the next big thing. We must be prepared to do the hard yards of relationship building. Change in political thinking and practice is rarely fast, but we must believe that the mustard seed will eventually produce fruit. There is also something of sacrifice and death about that seed. We will not necessarily be lauded for what we do, in fact it may not be noticed until generations after we are gone, but unless a grain of wheat falls to the ground and dies. . . .

So are we ready for the long haul?

Replication

We should be encouraged because thankfully this slowly replicating, sprawling DNA of the kingdom is not ours. It is God's. Incredibly, each of us is formed with divine DNA inside us. We are made in the image of God. Every tree has within it the potential to start a forest. The seeds are there. Every human has within them the potential to start a movement. The seeds of reproduction are there. The kingdom is unstoppable because it is in our DNA no matter how much we try to suppress it, by choosing the easier paths of disengagement and complaint. Those moments of slow growth happen with every moment of righteousness and justice. They happen every time we choose the King's way rather than the easy way.

Ask yourself why you joined any given movement. It probably wasn't the impressiveness of the website, or an eloquent piece of writing. It was probably a person. You knew a living, breathing, flesh and blood human being who gave you the nerve to sign up. Knowing someone who was already involved and knowing that they were not mad (well at least not totally mad!) is usually the key element in someone joining anything.

Relationship deficit

We also know that this kingdom will spread because our political system is crying out for integrity, creativity and vision. All across the country this vision is being shown by believers who are finding creative ways to tackle the challenges in their neighbourhoods. Whether it is befriending schemes for pensioners, or debt counselling programmes for those in fear of the bailiff, or lifeskills classes for at-risk teenagers, the church is stepping up. That energy is already starting to feed through into the political realm and we have the privilege of being part of that transformation.

So as we attempt to influence the political realm, let's remember again, it's a long haul because our God is a God of relationship. In his very essence, God is a team. He cares as much about his mission in us as his mission through us. But relationships take time and relationships take effort, especially if they are being formed with people who we may well disagree with on some things. That is the road less travelled. As humans we generally form tribes and stick with the folks who won't challenge us, but transformation happens when we stick our necks out beyond those comfort zones, to not just say something and run away, but to build relationships.

We have what I would call a relationship deficit. People draw people to a movement, but as Christians we are still isolated. We have allowed the separation of the church from the rest of society to happen. We have allowed the spheres of life to float off like a broken Newton's cradle.

A perfect example of this is the sphere of economics. I will never forget sitting in a meeting in Lambeth Palace in 2008. Rowan

Williams, then Archbishop of Canterbury, had invited some of the key players in the banking and financial services industry to tea. The seismic events of the global economic crash had taken place just a couple of months before. I was hoping it would be a kind of group confession. The CEOs of a range of banks and other financial agencies (who will remain nameless) were sitting around the meeting table. The opening gambit was thrown by Mr. A. He said, 'We've got to remember that this is not a moral crisis, it is an economic crisis.' Eyebrows were raised by some (including the Archbishop, whose eyebrows are better than most), but still silent politeness reigned. Mr. B chipped in, 'Indeed, we have to realise that in the last thirty years there have been very few losers. The only losers are those as yet unborn.' At this point, I and others simply couldn't hold ourselves back. How could they not see that that was a moral statement? That the fact that it was all right to mortgage the future of our children was not a moral decision? As you can imagine, a sturdy discussion on the need for ethics in the world of economics ensued. Then another bank chief stepped in. 'Well, it's all very well to talk about applying ethics to economics, but we are so multicultural now, it's almost impossible to know which ethics to apply!'

My chin was on the floor at this point. These gents (interestingly, they were all gents) were meant to be at the top of their trade, but they were talking at the intellectual and philosophical level of some of the kids on our estate. They really couldn't see beyond their immediate turf.

What was worse was that this was what they were saying just months after the most embarrassing indictment of their system in living memory, while sitting in a room in Lambeth Palace opposite the Archbishop of Canterbury. Goodness knows what they were saying six months earlier in a boardroom at the top of a Canary Wharf skyscraper!

It was the scariest evidence of groupthink caused by a silo mentality that I had ever seen. These people were obviously only talking to other people like them, or if they were talking to others, they were only *listening* to people who were just like them. We are also often guilty of this in the church.

The carnage happened because the only people that were allowed to speak into the world of economics without being sneered at were economists. Every sphere needs outside wisdom or it will descend into self-service, including the church. We are desperately in need of people who will straddle the worlds of the church and economics, the church and the media, and especially for our context, the church and politics. We need people who will be able to speak the language of both spheres, and do a job of translation between them.

However we need to encourage these straddlers fiercely because as any straddler will tell you, it's an uncomfortable place to be! When you have your feet on two mountains, there is only so far up either one you can get. This is not an ideal career path for advancement. From a financial and a status point of view, being a straddler is not a good move. You will spend more time in the shadows than in the limelight. But you will do some important kingdom work.

That is why we who are called to this slow, mustard-seed, uncomfortable, straddling experience need each other. That is why Christians in Politics exists. We need to support and pray for one another. I see that happening to an amazing extent with the Future Candidates groups from each party. From each other and God, they glean the energy to keep going when things are tough. When they have knocked the 300th door that day, they know that someone who understands is only a phone call away. When they have been excoriated at a public meeting, they are reminded that their identity doesn't depend on what others think of them. Am I selling this to you? I want to be honest, rather than a salesman. This is a tough road, but a crucial road, and you should see the fireworks at the end of it!

Clan

We are in this to do it together. We are going to work and campaign for one another rather than be obsessed with our own strategy. The candidates we train are sick of hearing me quote the old African proverb – 'If you want to go fast, go it alone. If you want to go far, go together.'

They are also sick of me asking them, 'Who is your clan?' Often they will come to me with hopes and dreams of becoming a Member of Parliament or a local councillor. My first question is always to ask them who is supporting them on this mission. Those who are talented and ambitious are also often those who tend to do things on their own rather than trust others to do anything, because generally they can do it better. A crucial lesson for these folks is that firstly, that isn't a kingdom method and secondly, in the political world that will only get you so far before you drop dead from exhaustion.

I will say, 'You need four or five people who will pledge to stick with you through thick and thin.' They will be people who will support you financially, practically and prayerfully. They will hold you accountable and encourage you in the darkest hours (because there will be dark hours). It is much better to build this clan before you even start because they will then have some shared ownership of your calling. They will offer wisdom on its direction, and already feel a sense of buy-in when you later ask for help. They will feel like it is also their thing. Too often I have seen people do everything themselves, like lone rangers, then start peppering people with requests for help as soon as they need to deliver lots of leaflets or make lots of phone calls. Ideally you want to get to the point where one of your clan can't stop themselves from organising that for you when the time comes, because they feel so much a part of it and believe so strongly in it.

The clan-building is also important because it provides a useful hurdle. If you cannot convince four or five people who love you dearly that you should be stepping forward into public leadership, then your chances of convincing the fifteen or twenty you will need for your team to follow you are slim. The chance of convincing the hundred or so local party members to select you will be slimmer still, and the hope of convincing 70,000 people in a constituency to vote for you may be nigh on impossible. These stages are useful tests of leadership. These filters can pretty quickly ascertain whether someone is made of the right stuff for public leadership. I don't just mean great communication skills or intelligent insight into issues, though those are important. More than anything I mean character and charisma whereby without even trying too much, people want to follow you. You can motivate and encourage, and your heart is to serve. You may well be already thinking of people like that who you know. Why not text them and suggest they utilise their gifts in public leadership? Or perhaps look in the mirror and tell yourself the same thing.

The other important thing about building a clan is that the journey is suddenly not just about you. The reality in many campaigns for public office is that they fail! There are far more people who want to be elected than can be elected. The political roadside is strewn with the bodies of those who have tried and failed. I have seen many believers do it with absolute integrity and excellent strategy, yet fail to be elected. This is not an exact science. Bearing in mind the level of commitment needed to the process, this is not a small consideration. People sometimes move house and give over years of their lives to being selected or elected in a certain area. I remember one of our brightest young candidates sitting in the Terrace Tea Room in Parliament and saying to me with a pained expression, 'What if it all comes to nothing? What if I don't get selected? I will have wasted two years for nothing! I'm not sure I can risk that.'

But if it's not all about you, then suddenly there is another perspective. If you build a clan then you are simultaneously discipling a crew of people into this form of public leadership. Many others who will follow you may pick up the bug. This has happened many times in my relatively short time in politics. Folks who have been willing volunteers a few years previously find themselves standing for office. They learnt their trade on someone else's campaign. They discovered a knack for conversation and a passion for neighbourhoods. They realised their need for God's help in the stretching process and it made their faith more alive. They have seen local issues like bins and dangerous dogs get sorted out along the way. But more than anything else they pick up a sense of God's heart for people and for government. With all this also going on, whether or not someone gets elected becomes less of an issue. God calls us to show up, not necessarily to win. (Though I think it is good to try to win!) In any campaign there is always so much more going on than the mere statistics of winning and losing. Areas are impacted by the campaigns which occur in them as well as by the people who end up winning. These campaigns decide the nature of public discourse for long periods of time – sometimes up to three or four years. That is significant public leadership you will be involved in, whether or not you win!

So here are some practical steps, which may not necessarily flow in this order, though often they do. It may help to see them through the lens of a missionary preparing to go overseas. This 'mission' is no different and the steps are similar.

Pray. Discern in which direction God may be leading you. In this area, God often guides people as much through relationships as through ideological resonance with a party. See where he is opening doors and opportunities.

Join A #Restore group in your area. These are springing up as Christians begin to take seriously their responsibilities to their local communities. Each gathering starts by brainstorming the needs of local communities and moves on to prayer and planning political and direct action.

Find your passion. Are there particular areas in which you are already expert? Perhaps based on your profession, or an agency you volunteer with. Or is there a need/injustice or principle that needs someone to champion it? To keep going in the tough times, you need a passion deep in your guts. You also need to be clear about how your theology informs your thinking about policy. Then you will have steel in your spine when the wild winds of the media and opposition blow.

Learn the language. Get informed about policy debates through books, websites, and training programmes recommended by Christians in Politics on our website. Theos (www.theosthinktank. co.uk) and other organisations provide fantastic online and offline resources that enable you to think about political issues. There are myriad blogs, which feature articles by members of the different political groupings. These are essential (but at times frustrating) reading for those who want to learn the language of the new culture. They will also lead you to live debates and meetings where you can hear actual human beings discuss the challenges facing the country. You will be amazed how quickly you will feel you have something to contribute. I cannot underline enough how being part of a church which is engaged in its community prepares you very well for political life.

Join a party. The websites of all parties make it easy to join online. You will be contacted by the local organisers in your vicinity. You will be surprised how quickly you are invited to all manner of events. As you get involved as a local activist; you will find you can have much more influence working from the inside. In a typical constituency there are 75,000 voters, 300 party members (though sometimes far fewer) choosing the candidates everyone gets to vote for and 10,000 Christians sitting on the sidelines. You can have a huge impact on who ends up on the ballot paper. If your primary frustration with politics is that 'there's no one that I'd want to vote for', then here is your chance to change that!

Join the Christian group within that party. Again it's very easy to do online. You will be able to attend prayer gatherings, policy discussions, training sessions and action days.

> www.christian-conservatives.org.uk
> www.christiansontheleft.org.uk
> www.ldcf.net

Get in touch with us at info@christiansinpolitics.org.uk for help in connecting with Christians in the other parties.

Find your clan. Who are the people who will support you on this journey? Find them.

Pray together. The fun is only just beginning.

Please remember that we are not for a second saying that the party route is the only way to go. It will not be the right route for some people. As we said earlier, others are called to more specific research roles or lobbying, but for too long as Christians we have gravitated more towards those roles, leaving the kingdom distribution of resources very skewed. (Remember the 90%/10% difference.) This book exists because we don't seem to have trouble adding to the 90%. That will continue to happen, and that is great. This book is part of trying to create a responsible, relational funnel to help folks get involved on the inside to add to the 10%. Also, within a party, not everyone is called to be a candidate. There are a huge number of roles, as volunteers or paid staff. You could be organising the logistics of door-knocking. You could doing graphic design for leaflets. You could be building websites. You could be co-ordinating prayer support. You could be raising money. You could be writing policy briefings. You could be liaising with the media. The possibilities are endless.

There are loads of great resources to help you explore your political leanings and the whole idea of politics on the Christians in Politics website www.christiansinpolitics.org.uk. There you can find excellent resources such as a four-week Bible Study course to do with your small group (with practical actions included), videos, theological background essays, and other inspiring stories of those who have already got involved. You can even take part in a quiz that will tell you which iconic political figures would be in your fantasy cabinet, based on how you answer certain questions. It was certainly very revealing to me!

This is what Steve Webb (Liberal Democrat MP for Thornbury and Yate) said about the resources.

> Politics is more than just voting occasionally. The Christians in Politics resources are provided to inspire and equip Christians to get involved more deeply in public life. The Bible clearly shows us that we are to be concerned for our neighbour. Through the resources we can find practical ways to express this responsibility in the sphere of politics. Our democracy offers the opportunity

and privilege of serving our local communities and the nation. We should never take this for granted. It's important for Christians to understand that the freedoms that we all enjoy come with a cost, and that our involvement is vital for their preservation. There has been an acute need for this kind of resource of broad engagement. I hope Christians make good use of it.

It is possible

Possibly the best way to encourage you that it is possible to build a clan within politics is to tell you about mine. We found one another around the edges of various Labour party gatherings. Someone knew someone who knew someone who knew someone. About twenty cups of coffee, a few curries and a lot of emails later we had bonded. But God has made it clear to us over the last few years, as we have gathered to pray into the left side of politics, that more than anything what we need to be is a family.

When people come together who have similar passions, the temptation is to spend most of your time discussing your latest ideas, mutual acquaintances or strategies to take the nation. For us we love talking about politics in general and of course our frustrations with the Labour party. But that can often waste time when we should really be praying for one another, seeking God, and crying out for his will to be done in the political realm.

Even more importantly we have learnt that being involved in the world of politics is a battle. There will be plenty of opportunities for discussing policy at innumerable events. There will be plenty of opportunities for networking with other fascinating people. But there are a very few places where people can come to have their wounds bandaged up. There are very few places where people can feel safe enough to fall apart, and confess how difficult it all is. There are few places where others will have the time, care and expertise necessary to meaningfully keep you accountable.

I have come to believe that missional communities of believers in every walk of life are very important to seeing kingdom advances in those spheres. I think nearly all of us involved in our group would say that we would not still be involved in politics if it were not for the support of one another. Being family means much more than just meeting every so often. It means sharing life. It has meant attending funerals of loved ones. It has meant cooking meals. It has meant counselling and hospital visiting. It has meant long journeys to grey places to support lost causes. I am convinced that kingdom change happens when we have sacrificial levels of commitment to one another.

My permission to do the job I am presently doing came through the backing of this clan. There was a coincidence of prophetic words that I could not ignore. At any time of the day or night I know they are available for emergency prayer or wisdom. We are not part of an organisation. We do not have a specific agenda, save 'your kingdom come, your will be done in politics'. These relationships are deeper than most because we are sharing a battle. You can never develop that depth by just meeting up for the sake of meeting. Anyone who has been to war or played in a sports team often reports that sort of depth. It is the sort of deep understanding that my wife reports with other mums sharing the joys and struggles of early parenting. The bond is palpable.

So I ask once again. Who are your clan? Who is going to walk with you through this adventure? Who are your peers who will hold you accountable and pick you up when you fall? Who are the team that will be swept up in the vision, giving you practical, prayerful and financial support, but may also be discipled along the way? Jesus sent the disciples out in no less than groups of two, and often there were a lot more. I am tired of hearing the desperate cries of lone ranger Christians who are running out of fuel because they have launched into a project on their own. It is often easy to create the appearance of a team (getting an email group to pray for you for example) without actually submitting yourself to the discipline of being accountable to others. But building a team takes effort and leadership. It is, as we have mentioned, the first test of your leadership. That's where the leadership has to start. And by God's grace, who knows where it may lead?

17

SHOWING UP: ORDINARY PEOPLE

The following are snapshots of some more ordinary believers who are showing up. I'll let them tell their own stories.

Jemima Bland

Jemima is the Liberal Democrat 2015 parliamentary candidate for East Worthing and Shoreham. She spends most of her week in the Westminster office of John Pugh MP. Her dog is a faithful companion on coastal campaigning days.

'Having worked in the Middle East, I'm motivated by the opportunity to take part in a democratic system that has become a model for democratic systems across the world. I want to help make our democracy a better reflection of our population, by getting more people of different backgrounds and cultures involved.

I'm a Catholic and the principles of Catholic Social Teaching have been important in thinking about the relationship between faith and politics. It's a practical philosophy. It's about human dignity and creating a connection between the individual, their suffering or their aims and ambitions, and the larger scale decision making that politics involves. There is room for Christian values to infuse Christian thinking about politics further – from community action to things like how we can build a stronger economy and a fairer society.

My faith is a private space in which I get to think about what is important. That's what prayer is, that's what going to church is about. It's not an easy space, it's quite a demanding one.'

Follow Jemima *@JemimaBlandLD*

Suzy Stride

Suzy Stride is the Labour 2015 parliamentary candidate for Harlow. When she's not on the campaign trail she can be found working for City Gateway, a charity striving to combat youth unemployment in east London.

'My upbringing and my family have been very influential in my decision to get into politics. I was brought up in Tower Hamlets on a council estate. When I was a child we would have Christmas dinner with my grandparents and all their friends. It's only recently that I realised [these friends] were homeless people they fed and clothed. It's about giving people dignity – they should be at the table with us. If your heart doesn't break for these things, I don't know what Bible you're reading – or what God you know.

I worked hard and got into Cambridge. But while I was there, something was always churning in my stomach. I had been able to realise my potential, but what about all the people I knew who weren't able to fulfil theirs? We know where some kids are going to end up [even] when they're in their mother's womb, and it's just not fair. I believe we need a government that levels the playing field.

I'm inspired by Clement Attlee. He went to a private school and then to Oxford, but the thing that transformed his life was that he went to Stepney and served at a working-class boys' club. He saw the reality of their lives, and it opened his eyes. We need to go and serve people and find out about their lives. Working for City Gateway keeps my feet on the ground; in one week I could be teaching a classroom of kids on one of the poorest estates in the country, and have a meeting with Ed Miliband.

Wherever you see Christians fighting for social justice issues – for me, that is evidence of God at work. I sometimes get frustrated that Christians who contact me always want to know about certain issues, and that's OK, but I look forward to the day when they are asking me about youth unemployment and council estates.

There's a lack of political education in schools, which fosters a lack of interest in politics. People think that all the parties are the same, and all politicians are the same – especially because they all look and sound the same. We need more people who've got out there and got their hands dirty, not just those who have been in the Westminster bubble.'

Fiona Bruce

Fiona Bruce has been the Conservative MP for Congleton since 2010. Before becoming an MP she was a businesswoman, solicitor and councillor.

'For me, politics is a calling. I didn't study politics, nor was anyone in my family involved in it. But I looked at the world my two boys were growing up in and felt it could be so much better. We all have a choice; we can stand on the sidelines or get involved and try to make a positive difference. Being able to make a difference in someone's life is the best part of the job.

Political involvement is a privilege and a high calling, because it's about the character of a nation. But unfortunately, poor character on the part of a number of individual parliamentarians recently has led to understandable public disillusionment. The challenge for us now is to win back the public's trust and confidence – it is, and will be, a long, hard road, but we must try.

I've been inspired by Lord Alton of Liverpool – perhaps better known as David Alton – who has led the pro-life work in Parliament for many years. It's a subject I am deeply concerned about and actively engaged in as co-chair of the All-Party Parliamentary Pro-Life Group. He is also the chair of the All-Party Group on North Korea, the country with the most religious persecution on earth, and it is a privilege to support him as vice chair.

The first thing I do when I get into the office is to pray. God gives me the energy to do what is a very demanding job.

Tim Farron

Tim Farron is now the President of the Liberal Democrats and has been MP for Westmorland and Lonsdale since 2005.

'I saw a re-run of the "Cathy Come Home" documentary when I was 14 and it moved me to tears and prompted me to join 'Shelter' the campaign for the homeless. Two years later I joined the Liberals largely out of a further developed sense of anger at the injustice that I saw around me in the north of England and (at the time of Live Aid) overseas. I was 18 when I became a Christian and I wondered for a while whether politics wasn't a rather grubby Godless world for a new Christian – but I look back and see that God led me to stay put and to stand up for what is right and to be a witness for him in my life as an activist. I don't know whether I ever really thought I would become an MP, but I know God put me here for a reason, to serve him and to make use of my Z-list celebrity status to promote the gospel in my own constituency and further afield.'

David Burrowes

David Burrowes has been the Conservative MP for Enfield Southgate since 2005. Before this, he was a criminal justice solicitor and a local councillor. He led the parliamentary opposition to the Marriage (Same Sex Couples) Bill. Between work and spending time with his wife and six children, he avidly follows the fortunes of Arsenal Football Club.

'I went to university with Tim Montgomerie [founder of Conservative Home, now comment editor at The Times] and together we started the Conservative Christian Fellowship. It was at a time (under Thatcher) when the idea of being a Christian and a Conservative was being challenged.

Christians are wary of getting involved in party politics and instead align themselves to Christian organisations or single-issue groups. But we have to be careful that we don't become an isolated bubble. We are a society based on numbers; unless you have the numbers, people won't have a represented voice.

Family breakdown is one of the biggest challenges facing our society. It has a huge social and financial impact. As a lawyer I saw the effects of this; those involved in crime are increasingly affected by fatherlessness and the lack of intergenerational role models. The identity of men and women in the context of family life is under attack. It's not just an old 1950s version of society. It's not about being squeaky clean. It's about standing up for traditional family values as an issue of social justice.

God is involved in every second of my life; he's in control. As a politician you can spend your time fire-fighting throughout the day, but through the Word and through fellowship with other Christians you can have a perspective that has greater value, and not dictated by the 24-hour news cycle. Seeing things through God's eyes and trying to be more like Christ creates – hopefully – a wise perspective as well as a security and identity that isn't dependent on power or approval.

Enoch Powell said that 'all political careers […] end in failure'. I'm ambitious for issues, but career-wise … if I were to have a career adviser tell me how to endear myself to the Prime Minister, I imagine it wouldn't involve opposing him on a key issue that he's personally very committed to. Some good advice I received early on was that it's a marathon, not a sprint – which means concentrating on issues and principles, which you can represent on the backbench, as a minister or as a campaigner.'

Follow David *@davidburrowesmp*

We finish our journey together with a prophetic vision and a prayer. Please join with us in this prayer and in this mission.

EPILOGUE

2020 vision

So, I'm praying and asking God to reveal what he wants to bring to pass in the realm of politics. I feel an ever so kind kick up the backside as I realise that he already has. He has planted this stuff inside many people the length and breadth of this country. As church members have encountered poverty and dysfunction during community action or international trips, their natural curiosity has led them to ask, 'Why are things the way they are?' They're not satisfied by the *status quo*. They're not satisfied with mere charity that allows us to feel we've done the right thing, without effecting long-term change. Having heard so often the adolescent cry of, 'It's not fair!' they're learning that injustice is often structural as well as personal. These facts are leading them to the natural conclusion things won't change while Christians are just shouting about them from the sidelines, rather than getting on the pitch.

I write this from the midst of a party headquarters in full knowledge of expenses scandals and Westminster elitism, so my glasses are not rose-tinted; this is not naïve dreaming, but genuine vision. God has promised to redeem and restore all of creation, and politics is merely the way we organise ourselves in the midst of it. God's perfection is the future. It will happen. The only question is how soon. You can be certain that we're the ones who will be the limiting factor, not God. Yet, we have the privilege of being partners with him in his project of 'making all things new.'

So here we go. In 2020 I can see that ...

Churches are missional in their DNA. People are continually serving their communities. They understand that this is a vital part of the discipleship deal, rather than a fun summer extra. Engagement with friends and community is breaking their hearts and forcing them to their knees. It's also highlighting where broken lives are a product of a broken society, so action is required not simply to mend individual lives, but to mend the context in which they attempt to grow.

Young people are at the leading edge of an eschatological shift that has spread to the whole church. They see themselves as partners in God's restoration and redemption of all things and agents of the kingdom in the here and now. At gatherings people are commissioned to bring heaven on earth, rather than cajoled into buying an escape ticket for heaven. They're ruthless in their desire for justice and righteousness to burst forth in schools, parks, youth clubs and the Internet. They refuse the old 'either/or' of denominational or ecclesiological boundaries in favour of 'both/and'. They are just as comfortable lobbying a supermarket to pay fair wages as they are praying for miraculous healings in the aisles of that supermarket. And just as comfortable speaking in the town hall as a local councillor as they are speaking in tongues in a brightly coloured prayer room.

Thus, local Conservative, Liberal Democrat, Labour, Green, SNP and other parties' branches are flooded with young Christians who always hold the kingdom above any political ideology, yet realise the need to find common cause, to engage and debate. They are building relationships that don't allow them to be pigeon-holed as 'crazy people'. They are listening and learning. They are serving and giving. They are blessing new friends, surprising them with gifts of fairly-traded chocolate. They are invaluable because they turn up on time for meetings and they do what they say they will do before the next meeting. People can see evidence of 'the yeast working through the dough', because there is a renewed integrity and enthusiasm about politics. They refuse to make politics about personality or abuse people just because they are from 'the other side'. They campaign and make their case on the doorstep and on social media with a smile and a listening ear. This exposure to the reality of people's lives breaks their hearts and inspires much prayer as they walk around estates and suburbs.

It is as normal for a Christian young person to be pursuing a life in politics, as it is for them to aspire to being a worship leader. This calling is being affirmed and given space to grow. People are astounded that MPs are working in rehabilitation centres and giving away so much of their money to good causes. The days when they were claiming expenses for garden gnomes are long forgotten.

Worldwide attention is focused on Westminster because MPs are being miraculously healed in the corridors of power and legislation that 'speaks up for those who cannot speak for themselves' is being enacted.

So how could this have come to pass?

Everything shifted when people started to see *politics as mission*. When we put politics in that part of our brains and hearts, we started to understand. In the same way that we would encourage, pray for, emulate, visit and support a missionary, we began to act like that towards those whose mission field was politics. Things changed when politics was presented as a counter cultural, subversive adventure rather than the maintenance of the Establishment. Things changed when we realised that we had the privilege of participating with our Father in his mission of the redemption, restoration and reconciliation of all things to himself, including politics.

Things changed when we saw that politics could be just people serving people rather than themselves.

PRAYER

God of all government

God of all Government,
Send workers into the harvest field of political life.
Call your people. Not simply those who pay you lip service,
But those who hear your voice and know your name,

Those who will not serve two masters,
Those who will choose kingdom over tribe,
Those who are not ashamed of the gospel,
Those who will speak up for those who cannot speak for
    themselves,

Those who will seek justice, encourage the oppressed, defend the
    cause of the fatherless, and plead the case of the widow,
Those who will seek to reconcile more than separate,
Those who will seek to co-operate more than compete,
Those who will seek peace more than power.

Those who will choose your glory over self-promotion,
Those who will choose truth over expediency,
Those who will listen to the still, small voice more than the
    megaphone of the media,
Those who will care for the least of these, rather than genuflect to
    the greatest.

Those who find their identity and security in divine election more
    than election by man,
Those whose citizenship is in heaven, and whose primary
    allegiance is to another King,
Those who cannot help but speak of the reason for the hope that
    they have,
Those who know your grace for their failings.

Call out an army that will march on its knees in humility
To fight not just with the weapons of this world
But the invisible ammunition of your Kingdom.

AMEN

At a time when too many have given up on politics, Andy Flannagan issues a compelling clarion call for churches to grasp the opportunity to serve. In my work, I see no group or network better placed to do so. And he is right: there is the opportunity for our politics to be transformed, and for democracy to be renewed.

STEPHEN TIMMS MP

A book that powerfully challenges our misconceptions about politics and asks us not to stand on the side lines and moan, but to get involved.

PATRICK REGAN OBE, FOUNDER & CEO, XLP

Andy consistently provokes and inspires in equal measures. His passion to play his part in the mission of God shines through.

RUTH VALERIO, A ROCHA UK

Books about politics can often be worthy yet a little dull. This is far from the case with *Those Who Show Up*. Andy wears his humour and heart on his sleeve and by the end I would be surprised if you aren't signing up.

TIM FARRON MP

Andy is a poet, a troubadour and a master storyteller. His words are like incense, rising out of the muck and pain and poetry of the margins.

SHANE CLAIBORNE, AUTHOR AND ACTIVIST

Andy's passion, biblical insight and story-telling ability will convince even the most sceptical that they could and should be more than mere commentators on politics.

GARY STREETER MP

Those Who Show Up is essential reading for every church leader. It provides a compelling vision of how our churches can be beating hearts that fill their members with passion to take the gospel into all corners of society. This book has challenged me, caused me to pick up my Bible, opened my eyes to new things and inspired me to pray earnestly and seek more of God's will. It may well do the same for you.

GILLAN SCOTT, GOD AND POLITICS IN THE UK

The book helpfully busts many of the myths and excuses given by Christians for why they don't or can't get more involved in politics. From accepting the potential boringness of political meetings, to looking at whether we can engage with parties we disagree with *Those Who Show Up* makes a powerful case for engagement. One of the most common complaints is that politics is dirty and too difficult to engage in without compromise – this is turned on its head with the conviction running through the pages that this is exactly why we must show up.

DANNY WEBSTER, ADVOCACY PROGRAMME MANAGER, EVANGELICAL ALLIANCE

Christians cannot stand on the sidelines any longer where politics is concerned! We need to get actively and prayerfully involved to see transformation in our communities and nation. It is when we show up and engage with our world that we can influence what happens in our Nation and pray His Kingdom Come. I recommend this book as a prophetic call to engage.

DR JONATHAN OLOYEDE, CONVENOR OF THE NATIONAL DAY OF PRAYER AND WORSHIP

In many ways the 'How should I vote?' question can be an exercise in missing the point. By contrast, Andy Flannagan has written an engaging book about how a General Election can be an excellent opportunity to reflect on how we can be more intentional and effective in our political engagement.

Flannagan weaves a fascinating narrative from the stories of various people who are attached to all the major parties. Here are accounts of people who have shown up and been willing to get involved in the political process. What I particularly liked was that alongside some fairly spectacular stories of Christians being involved in politics there are also stories of people who have made a difference to their community without actually getting elected.

JOHN WOODS, INSPIRE MAGAZINE

Andy Flannagan deals compellingly with the various arguments voiced by Christians who are sceptical about getting involved in politics. He is impressively nonpartisan with sufficient cross-party examples and heartwarming stories to make you feel that his concern is for kingdom advance, whoever is engaged.

ANDY PECK, CHRISTIANITY MAGAZINE